THE
BEGINNER'S GUIDE
TO RUNES

THE **BEGINNER'S GUIDE** TO
RUNES

Divination and Magic
with the Elder Futhark Runes

JOSH SIMONDS

ROCKRIDGE
PRESS

For general information on our other products and services or to obtain technical support, please contact our Customer Care Department within the United States at (866) 744-2665, or outside the United States at (510) 253-0500.

Rockridge Press publishes its books in a variety of electronic and print formats. Some content that appears in print may not be available in electronic books, and vice versa.

Interior and Cover Designer: Carlos Esparza

Art Producer: Tom Hood

Editor: Vanessa Ta

Production Editor: Mia Moran

Author photo courtesy of © Meg McGovern Hamilton, Rodeo & Co. Photography

ISBN: Print 978-1-64739-916-0 | eBook 978-1-64611-051-3

R1

*I dedicate this book to Odin, the All-Father,
the Wanderer who sacrificed himself
upon the World Tree to bring us the magic
and mystery of the runes.*

Contents

Introduction

Each of us who finds the runes finds them for different reasons. We all approach the runes from different walks of life and for different reasons, but one main reason is true for all of us—we are all drawn to the runes for their mystery. We seek to better understand the Universe, the forces within it, and even ourselves, by understanding the runes. Whether you learned of the runes from your grandparents or from a book that just pulled your attention, you'll find a clear and concise understanding of the runes and what they can add to your life in this guide.

Personally, I discovered the runes after I took a DNA test! I knew nothing of my ancestry prior to taking a DNA test, and what I discovered in that test showed me that I'm mainly of northern European descent. I am a strong mix of Nordic and Celt, and that fact, along with other pieces of information I discovered through the DNA test, led me to research my family history and genealogy. What I discovered fascinated me further. While I was doing this research into my family's background, I stumbled across the runes, and as soon as I did, it felt very much like a language I didn't know I knew. I felt drawn to them like they were lost members of my family. Whether it's a cultural connection or you're simply drawn to them for their mystery, all are welcome to the runes and the secrets they have to share.

Interestingly, after digging into my ancestry, I found my last name "Simonds" is derived from Sir Richard Fitz-Simon, or "Son of Simon," founding Knight of the Order of the Garter and the great-grandson of Eleanor Plantagenet. According to the *Anglo-Saxon Chronicle*, a collection of records documenting the genealogies of the Old English or Anglo-Saxons, the Plantagenet family, along with many other royal English households, claim descendency from Woden (or Odin). That's right—my father's family is descended from a royal family that claims descendency from the Great Wanderer himself. Whether he was a real figure in history (as some suggest he may be) or not, I found this fascinating, especially because I had found and been enraptured by the runes long before I discovered this specific fact.

This long and wandering journey into my genealogy and ancestry led me to my current profession as a psychic medium. I use the runes in my one-on-one readings, relying on them to help me better tune in to the energies and spirits around a person. I truly give credit to my ancestors, as well as the runes, for helping me discover these gifts within myself. The runes pulled these gifts from me much in the same way Odin pulled the runes from the Well of Wyrd.

Even though ancient in origin, the runes apply today, given that they are symbols and tools that help us connect to the energies of the cosmos and better engage the mysteries of life. It is my hope that the runes help you discover the gifts within you, whether it's latent intuitive powers, artistry, athleticism, or anything else that lies dormant within you.

I began my journey with the runes by pulling one each day, in the morning. I would keep a rune journal that I would write in each evening, taking notes from different resources of some of the common themes shown by the runes. Then, I would take notes as to how I felt that rune presented itself over the course of my day—sometimes they're very literal, sometimes very figurative. This gave me a chance to watch for different patterns throughout my day, and I believe this practice helped me develop my intuition. I encourage you to do the same; keep a rune journal handy with this guidebook and take notes at the end of each day, or even during the day, as to how you believe that rune showed itself to you. Building a relationship with the runes and discovering how they show themselves to you is the most important way you can come to use them.

This is a book for beginners, and though there are many valuable resources on runes, I hope this book serves as a jumping-off point for you that you'll come back to again and again. You'll discover history about the runes, as well as in-depth explanations for each rune of the Elder Futhark and their uses in divination and magic.

But most of all, I hope the runes help you discover yourself.

How to Use This Book

What you hold in your hands is a guidebook, built around years of study and experience. To understand the runes, we must commit ourselves to a consistent study of their mysteries, while being humble enough to accept we'll never come to completely understand their vast, powerful layers of meaning and intricacies, but remaining curious and driven enough to want to try.

This book is divided into three sections. In the first, we'll discover the origin of the runes, learning exactly what they are. We will explore different types of runes, and we will journey with Odin as we learn of his quest to bring us the runes. In the second part, various practices with runes will be explored, from divination to actual magical principles. From making your own set of runes to introducing different rune spreads, this second section will be your go-to resource as you begin your journey with the runes.

The third section may be the portion of the book that you visit more regularly, especially as you expand your exploration with the runes. Here, you'll find Freya's Aett, Heimdall's Aett, and Tyr's Aett, the three groupings of eight runes each. Each rune will be introduced with a guide to help you learn how to pronounce it, what it's known as in various other Rune Poems, and the keywords and definitions associated with it.

This guide is meant to be exactly that: something that helps you along on a journey. Feel free to read this book in any order you would like. Each of the three sections of the book—Rune Origins, Rune Practices, and Rune Meanings—is written in such a way that you can read it individually or read them all consecutively.

Thank you for taking this journey with me. I'm excited to be your guide.

PART ONE

Rune Origins

Let's dive together into the origins of the runes, from both a historical and mythological perspective. The word *rune* can only be found in Celtic and Germanic languages and can be translated as "secret" or "mystery." Runes have been with us for thousands of years, and they are found both in archaeological artifacts and in written lore, passed down through the years. They have been found on gravestones, spearheads, and jewelry, and on such materials as wood, bone, and metal. Runes are not only symbols of language, an alphabet of sorts, but also symbols of the great mysteries of the Universe.

Within the runes, we discover cosmological archetypes found throughout the world around us, as well as within the very fabric of humanity, the deep characteristics found within each of us. In the first chapter, you'll learn about the various runic rows found throughout history, including examples of artifacts discovered from antiquity, all the way through the modern revival of their use.

In the second chapter, you'll discover the ancient roots of the runes themselves, given to us through the mythology of the Norse people. You'll journey beside the All-Father himself as he discovers the runes and their power, and you'll learn of other powerful beings of Norse mythology and how they worked with the runes.

Most important of all, though, is that your journey with the runes will begin here. Just as Odin himself reached into the deep Well of Wyrd to bring forth the runes, so will you reach deep into this guidebook to bring the runes into your life.

CHAPTER ONE

The Runes

The runes are symbols representing the letters of an alphabet as well as symbols of magical use. In fact, well before the runes were used for communication, they were used for magical purposes. In this chapter, you will journey through the evolution of the runes themselves, from their very first iteration through the most recent versions of them. Runes have been used in magic, with purposes including cursing, blessing, and divination, as well as for communication, and as the cultures of the Norse and northern Europeans changed over time, so the runes changed with them. From the ancient tribal pagans to the Viking culture right through medieval and modern times, runes have been with us since the beginning of our human history.

The Runic Alphabet

The runes are one of the earliest known alphabets of the Germanic peoples of northern Europe. The word *rune* most likely comes from the Norse word *rún* meaning "mystery" and the Proto-Germanic word *runo*, meaning "letter" or "secret." Scholars are unsure of where, when, and by whom the runes were created, and although archaeologists know that the oldest runic inscription comes from about 50 CE, found on the Meldorf Brooch from Jutland, runes are likely far older than that.

Runes have strong, angular shapes and serve as letters and symbols, yet they are much more than that. Each rune is a pictograph with sharp forms, and though people can write and spell with them, they are also symbols that represent energies and concepts, both around us in the world and in the cosmos, and deep inside us. Runes were primarily found in the languages of Nordic countries, with each character marking a certain sound. One can invoke the powers and energies within each rune by speaking and drawing them, as well as meditating on them. Their most popular contemporary use is that of divination, or using them in spreads and castings, similar to those of Tarot cards.

In ancient times, runes were carved into hard organic surfaces such as wood and bone, and on other hard surfaces like stone and metal. They were used mainly to communicate, but were also utilized in magical and sorcerous purposes. As mythology tells us, the runes were brought to us by Odin, the chief god of the Norse pantheon, as he hung on the World Tree for nine days and nine nights, sacrificing himself. To know the runes is to know a relationship with Odin.

The runic alphabet is called the Futhark, which is an acronym for the first six runes in the Elder Futhark row. In historical times, runes were written in both directions, from left to right and right to left, and also upside down or inverted. The 24 runes of the Elder Futhark are divided into three *aetts* (Old Norse for "families") of eight runes each.

The Elder Futhark was made up of 24 characters. It was the first runic alphabet, but as the people of northern Europe migrated and cultures meshed, the Elder Futhark evolved into the Younger Futhark at the beginning of the Viking Age around 750 CE. The Anglo-Saxon Futhorc was developed in England, when the Elder Futhark was augmented to include 33 characters.

Most of our contemporary knowledge of the runes and their meanings derives from the three Rune Poems, historical texts from England, Iceland, and Norway. Each Rune Poem provides a short stanza about each rune in their Futharks. The Anglo-Saxon Futhorc is brought to life in the Old English Rune Poem, whereas the Younger Futhark is highlighted in the Icelandic and Norwegian Rune Poems. The *Poetic Edda* and *Prose Edda* are two collections of Old Norse writings that describe the origin of the runes, together serving as the most authoritative source of Norse mythologies.

The Elder Futhark

ᚠ   ᚢ   ᚦ   ᚨ   ᚱ   ᚲ   ᚷ   ᚹ

ᚺ   ᚾ   ᛁ   ᛃ   ᛇ   ᛈ   ᛉ   ᛊ

ᛏ   ᛒ   ᛖ   ᛗ   ᛚ   ᛜ   ᛞ   ᛟ

The Elder Futhark is the oldest version of the runes—both a system of magic and an alphabet for writing developed by the Germanic tribes during the Migration Period, a period of time that saw the movement of many invading peoples throughout Europe lasting from about the third to fifth century CE. The historical origin of the Elder Futhark runes has been contested by many scholars, but they are known to come from at least 50 CE, to when the oldest artifact portraying Elder Futhark runes has been dated. It is believed to have fallen out of use by the ninth century CE, when the Elder Futhark evolved into both the Anglo-Saxon and Younger Futharks.

The word *futhark* comes from the first six runes: Fehu, Uruz, Thurisaz, Ansuz, Raidho, and Kenaz, spelling out *f, u, th, a, r,* and *k*. The Elder Futhark runes are divided into three aetts, or groups of eight, containing a total of 24 characters. Runes have a cloudy past, because even though they can be used for communication, the early tribes of the Germanic people were largely illiterate; due to their use on gravestones, weapons, and sacred pieces of jewelry, it is believed they were used magically long before they were used for communication. Many scholars believe they originated from Italic alphabets, mainly the Etruscans', or the Latin alphabet itself, most likely due to trade routes. The sharp angles with which the runes were drawn were believed to have originated from the necessity to carve them onto hard materials, like wood, bone, or metal.

The Anglo-Saxon Futhorc

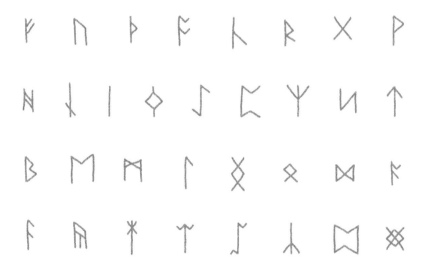

The Anglo-Saxon Futhorc came about as a continuation of the Elder Futhark rune rows. Instead of 24 symbols, the Futhorc (called so for the first six runes of the row) came to contain 33 runes. Between the fourth and sixth century CE, the Angles, Saxons, and Jutes invaded the British Isles and brought the Futhark along. The modification of the Elder Futhark to the Anglo-Saxon Futhorc was slow, first evolving to contain 26 runes, then eventually coming to contain 33 runes, reflecting the changing sounds of Old English, the language of the Anglo-Saxons.

The Anglo-Saxon Futhorc survives mainly due to the Old English Rune Poem, so it is seen as more of a written language with which to communicate, with less of a magical character. The Anglo-Saxon Futhorc seems to have evolved at the same time as the elusive Frisian Futhorc, with many scholars debating whether this runic row developed in England and moved to Frisia, a coastal region along the southeastern corner of the North Sea, or vice versa. Regardless, the Anglo-Saxon Futhorc was used in England until the 10th century or so, and its use ended with the Norman conquest in 1066.

The Younger Futhark

The Younger Futhark evolved over a period of many years, stemming from the Elder Futhark, eventually solidifying in form by about 800 CE, when the Viking Age began. The Younger Futhark was seen mainly in Scandinavia, eventually dropping eight of the original Elder Futhark runes to a shorter runic row of 16 runes. This is a peculiar development as the language of the Scandinavians was changing at this time, and unlike the runes dropping letters, their language was adding sounds, increasing the number of vowels from five to nine.

Whereas the Elder Futhark was a cherished secret among runemasters and the literate elite, this changed with the Younger Futhark in Scandinavia. Only 350 inscriptions of the Elder Futhark survive today; however, roughly 6,000 runestones and inscriptions survive of the Younger Futhark. The Younger Futhark inscriptions were first found in Denmark, sometimes called Danish or "Long Branch" runes. But soon another version developed, referred to as the Norwegian-Swedish or "Short Twig" runes, due to the differences in their written characters. The Younger Futhark was the primary means of written communication in Norse lands throughout the Viking Age, but eventually was replaced by the Latin alphabet by 1200 CE, due to the conversion to Christianity by the people of these lands.

Other Runes

Even though the Elder and Anglo-Saxon runes had become almost obsolete by 1200 CE, there were some versions that survived longer than that, and some versions that were brought forth by others who developed their own systems later on.

The Younger Futhark developed into the medieval system of runes in the early 13th century, after the introduction of Christianity. This was a Scandinavian system that developed from the Younger Futhark after the introduction of dotted runes toward the end of the Viking Age. These runes were in use until about the 15th century.

From the 16th to 19th century, there was a version known as the Dalecarlian runes, used in an isolated part of Sweden known as Dalarna. These were a mix of runes and Latin letters.

The Armanen runes came about due to Austrian mysticist and Germanic revivalist Guido von List and his publication in 1908 of *Das Geheimnis der Runen*, or "The Secret of the Runes." This set of runes contains 18 runes, closely based on the Younger Futhark, with two additional runes.

The Armanen runes were, sadly, utilized maliciously by the Nazi Party both as symbology and to further the abhorrent Nazi agenda of Germanic purity and genocide. Despite this history, they continue today in various branches of Germanic neopaganism; German occultist Karl Spiesberger and others revamped the Armanen runes after the war to remove racism and other negative connotations.

Ancient Artifacts

What we know of runes comes from the historical record of archaeology. The oldest known inscription of runes was found on the Meldorf Brooch, discovered on the west coast of Jutland, dated from the middle of the first century CE. As noted earlier, the runes were most notably known for their magical purposes, where "magical" connotes the use of means (such as charms or spells or, in this case, runes) believed to have supernatural power over natural forces, and then secondarily as a means of communication.

There are two main types of runic artifacts: fixed and mobile. The fixed types of artifacts include great runestones, "fixed" in place, which do not move and were never meant to move. The second type of runic artifact includes the mobile variety; these artifacts include weapons, jewelry, and other various objects that were carried and moved around by the people who carried them.

From what the archaeological record tells us, the use of runes on gravestones served two different purposes. First, they were used as curses to stop the destruction or desecration of the grave within which the stone was found. Notably, these gravestones were found *in* the graves, not on them. Also, the Norse were huge believers in the undead, and these gravestones were carved with runes to keep the inhabitants of the grave from rising as a *draugr*, or a zombie of sorts—the term literally translates to "again-walker." These beings reside in their graves, guarding the treasure that was interred with them in their burial mounds.

Runic artifacts of the mobile variety include drinking horns, boxes, buckles, and brooches, as well as weapons, tools, and amulets. Amulets would have served as talismans, worn on the body as protection or to bring about good fortune. Brooches served the same type of purpose, but were pins of a type meant to hold together cloaks or other pieces of fabric. Runic inscriptions appeared to have both a passive and aggressive purpose. First, the passive means would have been like those found on brooches, meant to bring about good fortune or luck. The more aggressive type of purpose would have been like those found on weapons or shields, meant to bring about great harm to enemies or protection to the bearer.

The uses of runes for both magical and divinatory purposes are found in historical texts, as well as in the classical lore of the *Poetic* and *Prose Eddas*. We know from the Roman historian Tacitus's account of the Germanic people that they used casting lots to read omens. The *Hávamál* also references Odin's mention of runes for divination, healing, and necromancy.

Modern Revival

Runes remained in use throughout Nordic countries in some form or fashion throughout all of known history. Whether they were used in the remote forests of Scandinavia, passed down from family to family, or simply used as a way of writing, they have remained, never completely dying out.

Christianity had an incredible stifling effect on the pagan ways of northern Europe. We see this in the outlawing of the use of runes, as well as specific laws written into existence to make illegal the use or possession of runes, seen as witchcraft. Yet, no matter how much these oppressive systems and regimes were determined to eradicate the runes, they were never fully successful. The power of the runes prevailed.

In the early 1800s through the 1900s, there was a revival of folklore and nationalistic movements in Scandinavia and Germany, and this led to a renewed interest in the runes. This included the aforementioned Guido von List and his Armanen runes, the use of which was perpetuated by the Nazi Party due to their association with Aryan supremacy and Germanic nationalism. Runes were strongly stained by this particular association, and even today, there is abhorrent use of runes among white supremacist groups and neo-Nazis.

Runes were also brought into popular culture by J. R. R. Tolkien. A professor and author, Tolkien showcased runes with his book *The Hobbit*. First published in 1937, the cover was ringed in Anglo-Saxon runes, and they were featured extensively as "Dwarf runes" in *The Hobbit* and its subsequent sequels.

The use of runes as a magical and divinatory tool was brought back into popularity in the 1970s, alongside the rise of Wicca and alternative, non-Christian spiritualities. Modern authors like Ralph Blum, Stephen Flowers (Edred Thorsson), and Freya Aswynn published books showcasing their uses and interpretations, bringing the runes to millions of people worldwide.

CHAPTER TWO

Runelore

What we know of the runes comes from two literary sources: the Rune Poems and the lore. The mythology and lore surrounding the runes come from two main sources, the *Prose* and *Poetic Eddas*, as well as various other sagas.

By studying the lore and mythology of the ancient Norse people, we not only learn of the origin of the runes, but we also discover the gods and creatures that brought them to us and showed us how to use them, including Odin's sacrifice upon the World Tree. As you'll discover in this chapter, the runes show up in many stories and myths from the ancient Norse, lending us just enough clarity and guidance to begin our journey of discovering them.

Norse Mythology

The Norse people of ancient times lived in a harsh, often unforgiving land. Prior to the Middle Ages, when most Norse converted to Christianity, they celebrated life with a pagan spirituality reflecting the difficult, yet beautiful, realities of the world in which they lived. The Norse system of spirituality wasn't a religion as much as it was a tradition, and at the center of that tradition were the stories that made up Norse mythology.

What we know of Norse mythology comes from two historic sources: the *Poetic* and *Prose Eddas*. Transcribed in medieval times, these texts include great poems and stories, including the *Hávamál*, or "The Sayings of the High One," directly attributed to Odin, from which we learn of the origin of the runes. These myths provided rich meaning to the lives of these ancient people, showcasing beautifully complex and terrifying creatures and gods, such as Elves, Dwarves, Giants, and deities like Odin, Thor, and Freya.

The ancient Norse knew there to be nine worlds, of which our world, Midgard, was only one. These nine worlds were connected by the World Tree, Yggdrasil, an ash tree that stood at the center of these nine worlds. Yggdrasil linked all the worlds, and if one was to travel from one world to another, they would do so on the World Tree. Under one of the roots of Yggdrasil was the Well of Wyrd, where the three Norns dwelled. The Norns are often compared to the Three Fates of Greek mythology, a trio of maiden, mother, and crone who acted as the "Weaving Sisters," spinning, measuring, and cutting the fates of all beings. Odin is credited with discovering the runes, and he did so by hanging from the World Tree for nine days and nine nights, over the Well of Wyrd.

There were two main groups of gods and goddesses: the Vanir (the fertility gods) and the Aesir (the sky gods). Though Odin is the chief god among the Aesir, who resided in one of the nine worlds known as Asgard, Freya of the Vanir is the preeminent goddess of the Norse. Freya was the very first Seidr practitioner, the ancient Norse fertility and earth magic that was known for its ability to both curse and heal.

The Aesir attempted to murder Freya, and because of this, a great war broke out between the Aesir and the Vanir; that war lasted only so long before each side tired of it and came to a truce. As was the custom, each side paid tribute to the other by sending members of their tribe to the other side. Freya—along with her father, Njord, and her brother, Freyr—was sent by the Vanir to Asgard, where she became Odin's wife.

Though Odin is known for his shamanic and magical abilities, it was Freya that taught them to him. Odin was the Great Wanderer, known for his poetry, cunning skill in battle, and wisdom well before his journey to discover the runes; once he discovered them, they only added to his wondrous magic.

Odin

Since the dawn of history, humanity has worshipped countless gods and goddesses. From prehistoric cultures to modern religions, gods and goddesses have portrayed many different noble—and not so noble—attributes. We must remember, as we learn some of the mythology of the Norse, that their stories carry with them cultural values and context that might not make sense to our modern minds, just like many other myths from around the world. Foremost among the Norse was the god Odin, the chief god of the Aesir, known among both the Vanir and Aesir for his wisdom.

As we discover in the lore, the cosmos were created by the frost of Niflheim and the fires of Muspelheim (two of the nine worlds) coming together over Ginnungagap, the great void. As the flames melted the ice, Ymir, the first of the Giants, was born from the drops. Audhumla, a great cow, came forth from the frost as it melted, feeding Ymir with her milk and finding nourishment in the salt found in the ice. Her licking eventually revealed Buri, first of the Aesir gods. Buri's son, Bor, married Bestla, daughter of the Giant Bolthorn, and when Bor and Bestla came together, they had three children: Odin and his brothers, Vili and Ve. Ymir was slain by Odin and his brothers, who built the world from his corpse. After building the world, Ask and Embla, the first man and woman, were brought forth by the gods from two tree trunks.

Although Odin reigns over Asgard, he is known as the Great Wanderer. He ventures from the kingdom of Asgard, seeking wisdom and power. In fact, wisdom and inspiration can be said to be Odin's main goals. His name comes from two Norse words—*odr*, a word that might be translated into English as "inspiration" or "ecstasy," and *inn*, which means "the." Odr was a frenzied state of ecstasy, said to be so powerful as to be divine. Odin's name can be said to mean "The Ecstatic One" or "The Inspired One."

Odin is the patron god of rulers as well as outcasts. There may be no other god known to man as renown for how varied his interests are, nor how layered his character. Not only a god of war, Odin is also a god of poetry, said to only speak in poems. He sometimes appeared to men and women in full armor, ready to fight and lead his followers into battle, and sometimes he appeared as an archetypal wizard-type figure, in full cloak and wide-brimmed hat, carrying a walking stick. In fact, Tolkien's character of Gandalf was based on the character of Odin.

Odin has many familiar spirits around him, helping him in his duties to rule over the nine worlds. The Valkyries are female spirits, or maidens, known as the "Choosers of the Slain," sent to battlefields to choose the fallen warriors worthy of a place in Valhalla, Odin's great hall in Asgard. Odin has two attendant ravens, Huginn ("Thought") and Muninn ("Memory"), known to fly all over Midgard, bringing Odin back information of happenings. Odin also has two wolves by his side, Geri and Freki, both meaning the "ravenous" or "greedy." Perhaps Odin's best-known familiar spirit is Sleipnir, his great eight-legged horse, or "The Sliding One." Sleipnir could very well be considered one of his shamanic helping spirits, assisting his movement from world to world along Yggdrasil, the World Tree.

No matter how Odin appears to people, there is one characteristic that is consistent throughout all tellings of him: his singular eye. Odin was known for his primal drive for knowledge, seeking out wisdom and information to help increase his power. He would go through any trial, including his quest for the runes, to attain knowledge and wisdom. He would go through any physical trial to attain knowledge and wisdom, including gouging out his eye as trade and the torment he endured for the runes. The story of his quest for the runes comes from the *Hávamál*, specifically stanzas 138–141.

Sitting upon his great throne in the kingdom of Asgard, Odin spied the runes upon the roots of the World Tree, carved by the Norns. Odin's quest to gain the runes showcases his willingness to undergo unimaginable torment and pain to gain knowledge. Many scholars consider his journey to attain the runes as a shamanic initiation, a journey to access great wisdom.

Odin hung himself upon the World Tree, for nine days and nine nights, stabbing himself upon his great spear, Gungnir. After these nine days and nine nights, the ecstasy and inspiration of the runes showed themselves to Odin as he hung over the Well of Wyrd. Reaching down into the Well, Odin brought the runes up "screaming." Once he had knowledge of the runes, he cut himself down from the tree and revived himself with a drink of the Mead of Poetry.

Odin's story of obtaining the runes is just one of the many stories of Odin's quest for knowledge and wisdom. This is where we should all start as we journey to learn the runes. As we expect to gain knowledge of the runes, we should also expect to give up a piece of ourselves—our time, our effort, and, most especially, our devotion.

Sigrdrifumal

In the *Poetic Edda*, we find many myths and stories relayed to us about ancient Norse mythology. One of the most significant tellings in regard to runes and runic magic is that of *Sigrdrifumal*, a section of the *Poetic Edda* that details the meeting of Sigurth, a legendary Germanic hero, with the Valkyrie Brynhildr, identified here as Sigrdrifa.

Valkyries were Odin's attendant female spirits, or "Choosers of the Slain," the spirits who bring the souls of the chosen slain from battlefields to Valhalla, Odin's great hall in Asgard. Sigrdrifa means "driver to victory," or "victory urger." This poem deals specifically with Sigurth's journey to the top of the mountain Hindarfjall. Seeing a great light upon the mountain, he rode to the top to find a fortress with flags flying atop of it. He went into the fortress and found a person sleeping on the floor, fully armored. He removed the helmet and was surprised to find the person was a woman. Her chainmail was bound tightly to her skin, almost like it had grown into it, and upon cutting it open with his sword, Sigurth woke up Sigrdrifa, freeing her from a curse Odin had placed upon her. Odin had promised victory to a great warrior in a battle, and Sigrdrifa killed the warrior to whom Odin promised victory because his opponent had no help in the battle.

Sigurth asked Sigrdrifa for wisdom, if she were kind enough to share, of the nine realms. This part of the *Poetic Edda* brings us to a beautiful recounting of many magical ways to use runes.

> *"You should carve victory-Runes*
> *if you want to have victory.*
> *Carve some on the hilt of your sword,*
> *carve some on the middle of the blade also,*
> *some elsewhere on the sword,*
> *and name Tyr twice."*

This verse especially shows us that runes were carved into weapons and shields, and also possibly showcases the idea of bindrunes. This stanza gives us insight into the Tiwaz rune and how it can be used in battle. Being the first rune stanza, it also highlights how important battle was to the ancient Norse. The next stanza showcases something almost as important as battle to the Norse: beer.

> *"You should learn beer-Runes*
> *if you don't want another man's wife*
> *to abuse your trust if you have a tryst.*
> *Carve them on the drinking horn*
> *and on the back of your hand,*
> *and carve the Rune for 'N' on your fingernail."*

This is a curious stanza, and not just for the mention of infidelity, which is even more curious because later on Sigrdrifa advocates that Sigurth never encourage a woman's "looseness." This stanza shows us a very specific manner of how to use a rune magically: by carving it into our fingernails. The "N" rune referenced here is Nauthiz.

Later on, Sigrdrifa mentions childbirth, and how to save a woman's life while in the throes of childbirth:

> *"You should learn life-saving Runes*
> *if you want to save a woman's life*
> *when she is in the throes of childbirth.*
> *Carve them on your palm,*
> *and clasp them around your limbs,*
> *and pray to your family spirits for help."*

Also in this particular telling, we see mention of "wave-runes," used to save ships out on the "wild water." We're taught about healing runes, as well as speech-runes, used to prevent those who hate you "from taking vengeance on you." We learn about mind-runes, used to help us become wiser than any other man, and we learn of runes carved on shields.

Finally, Sigrdrifa recounts to Sigurth of the runes' great advice we could all live by as we learn the runes:

> *"The beechtree-Runes*
> *and life-saving Runes*

and all the beer-Runes
and the famous strength-Runes
will be of good use
for everyone who knows them
completely and correctly.
Use them, if you know them,
till the gods die."

The Runes of the Gods

Many students of the runes may find themselves frustrated when they begin to study them, especially if they do not have a guidebook like the one you hold right now. There seem to be many myths and poems from the ancient Norse, yet it seems that there aren't enough that help us discover the runes themselves. We can read the beautiful Rune Poems, and are fortunate to have them to help us understand each of the runes, and yet our journey to know the runes requires us to dig a little deeper. Though we only have a handful of poems and sagas that specifically mention the runes, we do have plenty of myths and stories that have to do with the gods themselves.

We must study the stories of the gods, the embodiments of the runes themselves, and in this way, we can better learn the runes and discover their mysteries. There are several runes that relate to the gods specifically: Ansuz is Odin's rune, Thurisaz is Thor's rune, Tiwaz is Tyr's rune, and Ingwaz is Freyr's rune.

With the story of Odin, we can better learn the mysteries of Ansuz, the rune of wisdom, breath, and communication. Odin is the "The Ecstatic One," or "The Inspired One," said to only speak in poems. Ansuz is a rune we can use to help us become inspired, especially around matters of communication.

With the story of Thor, we find the power that lies within Thurisaz. Thurisaz is the thorn—the thorn that protects and the thorn that pierces. It is Thor himself, yet also the Giants from whom Thor must protect us. Thurisaz is a rune of power and of force, a rune used when in need of defense, and a rune that shows us that we should be on the defense against powers greater than ourselves.

Tyr is one of the gods of whom we know very little. In fact, it seems that only one story survives from antiquity describing anything of substance about Tyr, and this is the Binding of Fenrir, the great wolf. We know that Tyr is a god of war and a god of fairness, cosmic righteousness, and law. Through the myth of Tyr and how he lost his hand to Fenrir, we can better come to understand Tiwaz, the rune of strength, truth, and justice.

Freyr is a fertility god, known for reaping his blessings upon those who worship him. Ingwaz is the great seed, a rune of new growth and male fertility, and many of Freyr's depictions show him as particularly masculine. In the study of Freyr's myths and stories, we can come to better understand Ingwaz.

There are also many correlations to be drawn between archetypes and characters within Norse mythology and lore and specific runes. We know Eihwaz, the 13th rune, to be the rune of the ash tree, and by coming to understand Yggdrasil, the World Tree, the Great Ash Tree, we can come to know Eihwaz better. We know Ehwaz is the rune of the horse and journeying. We can come to know Sleipnir, Odin's great eight-legged horse, through stories that recount his journeys with Odin. To better know Yggdrasil is to better know Eihwaz, and to better know Sleipnir is to better know Ehwaz.

In our journey to better discover and understand the runes, it is paramount that we develop a relationship with them made stronger by using them on a daily basis. Although personal experience with the runes should be your foremost tool, don't forget to read the lore and myths of the Norse, especially those specific to their gods. By studying their stories and coming to better know their struggles and victories, you will come to better know the runes, and eventually yourself.

PART TWO

Rune Practices

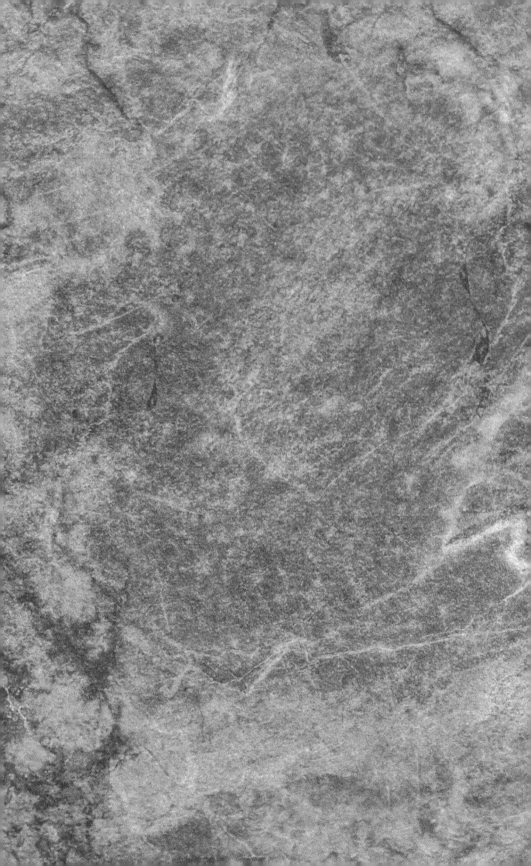

Runes have a rich history. There are archaeological finds and ancient texts that help illuminate how and when runes have been used, yet what is known must be only a small portion of what's been lost to history. Runes, though, have a way of permeating our very existence, no matter how much was lost to the tides of time. Runes are the primary threads in the fabric of reality, the tethers that hold all together, and they make themselves known throughout our daily lives. The powers they represent make up the building blocks of life, and because of that, they are much more than just a written language or grouping of symbols: They are indeed the fibers of the cosmos, found at the base of Yggdrasil.

The runes manifest themselves in our physical, emotional, mental, and spiritual selves, through the human qualities we manifest in our lives here on Midgard. They are intimately connected to the Norns, the three weaving sisters of Nordic faith, and they are the tools and teachings of Odin. Divination is likely the most frequently practiced runic magic. There are many methods of runic divination (in other words, to *reach to the divine* using the runes), from drawing a single rune to elaborate rune spreads or full castings of the entire Elder Futhark, and more.

Runes belong to ancient practices throughout northern Europe, magical practices including simple gestures like carving runes onto combs, and grander gestures, like erecting great stones, of tribute or methods of cursing and protection. The lore and archaeological records show us that runes were much more than a way to communicate, but also a way to engage with forces unseen.

Let's begin that journey, with great respect and gratitude for the powers that are the runes.

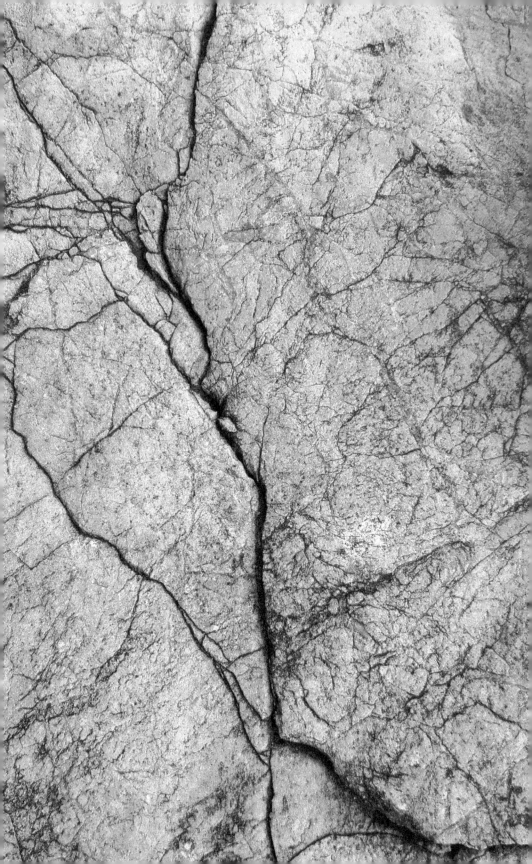

CHAPTER THREE

Runic Divination

Runes are symbols that represent the archetypal building blocks of creation, the great elements and energies
that coalesce and dance around us. They are keys to help
unlock our inner landscapes, as well as tools to help us
increase our own intuition. We can work with the runes to
find messages that can help guide us or warn us, tapping
into the wiser, hidden powers of the Universe. We can do
so in a variety of ways, most of them involving our own
set of rune stones with which we've built a relationship,
yet we can make do with runes written on slips of paper
in a pinch. Like anything else, the best way for you to find
results using runes for divination is to do so regularly. It's
vital to build a personal relationship with the runes, learning our own interpretations based on experience that we
can add on top of the classical, mythological interpretations found in lore.

Origins and Practice

We know the ancient lore of the Norse shares with us the story of Odin's discovery of the runes. It is a tale of sacrifice, of Odin's nine days and nine nights on the World Tree, speared in the side, before he brought forth the runes from the Well of Wyrd. In its own way, this simple act of drawing forth the runes from the well at the base of Yggdrasil was a divination of sorts, in that he was seeking knowledge and answers. Each rune represents great knowledge—knowledge that Odin would come to know as he brought the runes forth. This myth, as well as many other references in the *Poetic Edda*, shows us what we know of divination with runes.

One of our greatest sources of information about rune casting, or the "casting of lots," comes to us from Tacitus, Roman historian and author. In his work *Germania*, he shares with us an account of divination from the northern Germanic tribes of Europe circa the first century CE:

"For divination and the casting of lots they have the highest regard. Their procedure in casting lots is always the same. They cut off a branch of a nut-bearing tree and slice it into strips; these they mark with different signs and throw them completely at random onto a white cloth. Then the priest of the state, if the consultation is a public one, or the father of the family if it is private, offers a prayer to the gods, and looking up at the sky picks up three strips, one at a time, and reads their meaning from the signs previously scored on them. If the lots forbid an enterprise, there is no deliberation that day on the matter in question; if they allow it, confirmation by the taking of auspices is required."

Runic divination has certainly changed over the years, yet the reasons we turn to the runes have stayed the same: We're trying to find a deeper connection to the Universe around us, striving to find guidance and clarity via the subtle forces of reality around us, and yearning to connect to the spirits and gods that may bear influence on our lives.

Those who work to come in closer relation to the runes can use an elaborate casting ceremony like the one mentioned in Tacitus's *Germania*, or it could be just as simple as carrying pouches with them and pulling single runes as an answer to a question. Now, there are card sets that you can use in place of rune stones or chips, sold right next to Tarot and oracle cards, and people can download apps onto their smartphones that offer randomized rune pulls and rudimentary definitions.

No matter what way the runes present themselves, their energies are consistent in our lives, just like the elemental forces that make up the world around us. We use divination methods to help us today, just like our ancient ancestors before us, to find a clearer, wiser, and safer path through this world.

Principles of Runic Divination

Preferably when casting runes, you're doing so with a set that you've created and bonded with, but it's certainly not necessary. The magic of the runes exists in the runes themselves, not in the person who casts them. If you don't have access to a rune set, you can make do with pieces of paper. If you are going this route, if you're stuck in a pinch and need to make paper runes, try your best to do so with red ink, a traditional color that represents power and life force, and mimics the traditional practice of using blood to color runes. Blood is traditionally prized in esoteric workings as it connects directly to your inner life force, thus connecting your runes directly to your own essence. In our modern age, it is very easy to purchase runes, and though that may be your only option, it also causes us to lose the personal relationship that a hands-on creation can bring. Ideally, your rune set is one that you've created yourself, as explained in the sidebar on page 33, but if you don't have the resources or time, you can still go through a process of bonding with the runes you picked up at a store or online.

Whether we make our runes ourselves or purchase them, we must come in right relation with the materials the runes are made of, as well as the runes themselves. Tradition, as shown in Tacitus's *Germania*, calls for wood that's taken live from a nut- or fruit-bearing tree, yet downed wood is fine—as long as it's not rotted through. When taking wood from a tree, whether it's still on the tree and living or found on the forest floor, it is vital to make an offering to the spirit of the tree when you do so. This would be something as simple as leaving maple syrup, honey, or tobacco at the base of a tree if you're in North America, or you can use a special plant-based offering that's unique to the land you call home. If you would rather make runes out of stones, bones, antlers, clay, or any other material or resource that comes from the Earth, it is still important to make an offering to the spirit of the material with which you're working, just like the tobacco, honey, or maple syrup just mentioned. It is very important to give offerings to the spirits on which we call to be allies, as this shows we appreciate them and what they bring to us. This also sways them to be more helpful in our workings.

That spirit of offering is important to remember as you work with the runes. We should make offerings to the spirit of the materials with which we make our runes, but it is important to remember he who brought us the runes and to make offerings to him as well. To develop a relationship with the runes is to develop a relationship with Odin, the All-Father, and you can go far by making offerings to him. Offerings of mead and wine, bread and honey, are all treasured by the All-Father. This can be done inside on an altar, using a special bowl, cup, or plate, or outside in a natural space.

Whether performing a rune casting for yourself or someone else, it's always important to thank Odin for his sacrifice and ask him to lend wisdom and guidance to you, through the runes. Another important part of asking the runes a question is to blow into the bag or sack of runes before you shake them. This gets your *ond*, or life force, onto the runes so they can better meld with your energy, and thus provide you with the answer you need.

We seek out the runes to help us find our way through life, from very practical standpoints to more spiritual and esoteric ventures. This begins with consulting the runes, or simply asking them a question. When it comes to asking questions of the runes, it's important to keep your questions simple and to the point. If you have a complex issue to address, it's better to break it down into easy, concise questions, rather than one long, elaborate question. It is better to ask more simple questions than it is a few really elaborate ones. After you thank the runes and Odin, after you've blown into the pouch or sack of runes, you should concentrate and focus on the issue or problem for which you're seeking guidance, such as the beginning or ending of a relationship, or a crossroads in your career. Chant Odin's name nine times, slowly and with reverence, intoning his name to bring him close to the question for which you need clarity. Ask the question aloud, if possible; if you must ask the question silently, do so with the clearest and strongest inner voice you can find.

If you're reading for someone else and you feel comfortable doing so, have that person blow into the bag of runes to incorporate their ond into the runes before they're cast. It's not ideal to blow your ond onto the runes when pulling for others, as that might affect the casting. It is also your preference if you want them to draw their own runes, or if you're going to pull the runes for them. After all of this, the rune is pulled and consulted, relying on your knowledge, experience, and intuition to find guidance from the runes.

Making Your Own Set of Runes

As your runes will become your ally, a resource to consult and seek guidance from for the rest of your life, it's preferable that you make your runes yourself. This brings these ancient symbols into creation in a way that only you can and helps link your energy with theirs. Here you'll find basic instructions on how to create your own runes.

As mentioned, the traditional and ideal material for your runes is wood, preferably from a nut- or fruit-bearing tree. You can also use a variety of organic and earthy materials, such as stones, pebbles, and seashells of roughly the same size. If you use bone or antler, please do your best to make sure it's from an animal that died a natural death, or had a death of which you know. In any of these cases it's always important to make offerings to the spirits of the material you're working with. You will also want to have a bag in which to carry and store your runes, and though you can certainly buy one, again it's preferable to make one if you can. All of the principles we've covered so far about runes—using natural materials, making offerings to the spirit of the material with which you're making them—also apply to the creation of your rune bag.

There are several ways to inscribe runes onto your material of choice. Wood is the most versatile: You can carve into it, you can burn it with a wood-burning tool, or you can even paint it. Hard materials like bone or stones can be inscribed with a Dremel or other brand of rotary tool, or you can simply paint them. I believe the act of carving or inscribing adds another, deeper element to the creation of your lots, as it gives you more time to make them your "own," as well as to pour energy and intention into the runes as you make them. Also, when you inscribe or carve your runes, it gives you the chance to add more dimension to your casting lots, as adding ink, paint, or even traditional blood contributes more richness and depth to the runic characters. If you paint or stain your runes, you can add shellac as a protective layer.

What You'll Need:
- A material to inscribe your runes on—this can include wood, bone, stone, leather, clay, seashells, paper, or other material
- A natural dyeing medium: paint, ink, or blood
- Shellac or clear-coat spray for painted runes

(continued)

- A carving implement, a Dremel rotary tool, or a wood-burning tool
- Safety glasses
- A fine, thin paintbrush
- A sterile lancet, alcohol swabs, and a bandage, if you're working with blood, all of which are available at drugstores in the diabetic supplies section. (Do not draw blood from a vein—a fingertip will suffice and is much safer. Look up blood-drawing techniques for people with diabetes online to do this safely.)
- A first aid kit—as with any crafts requiring the use of power tools or sharp objects, it's a good idea to have one on hand

To create your runes, take a piece of base material, whether it's a piece of bone, wood, clay, or paper. Inscribe one rune into each piece, and as you do so, it would be a fantastic idea to chant or intone the name of the rune. Once they've been inscribed, whether it's through carving or burning, you can now dye, paint, or fill them with ink, paint, or blood. If you are not keen on using blood or other dyeing mediums, you can leave a rune as is if it's been created with a wood burner—the scorching of the wood burner will provide enough definition. If you are carving into a light-colored material, it will almost be necessary to fill the rune markings with a darker dye or paint to help define them.

Once you've created your runes, it is time to consecrate them. You can do this in a simple or elaborate ceremony, however you choose. You can time the consecration ceremony with astrological influences, or perform it on the night of the full or new moon, whatever your preference is. Follow your intuition as to the best way to consecrate your runes, but whatever you do, do it with reverence and gratitude in your heart.

A basic ceremony would include creating a circle of stones (representing earth) into which you would place your runes. Incorporate the other three elements into the ceremony as well, with a bowl of water to the left and a candle to the right. An offering of incense could go to the top of the circle of stones, indicating air and helping your wishes and intentions travel up to the gods and ancestors for their blessings. Place your runes in the center of the circle of stones, offer up words of gratitude, and ask for Odin and your ancestors to bless your runes. It would also be appropriate to have a bowl or plate nearby into which you can place offerings of gratitude. You can reference the works of Diana Paxson to find more detailed ceremonies, for both groups and individuals, along with other great books on runes in the Resources section (page 147).

No matter the kind of ceremony you come up with, it should go without saying at this point that it is important to bring offerings of gratitude to Odin, not only for his knowledge and sacrifice to bring the runes, but also for his help in guiding your hand in the creation of your lots. You can consecrate your runes individually or as a group, you can perform a single ritual to bless all the runes at once, or you could stretch out the ceremony for 24 days, celebrating and aligning to a rune a day. Meditate over each rune and say a prayer or blessing over it, asking that these runes help provide you with clarity and guidance.

Once they've been consecrated, be sure to carry them with you for at least 24 hours, and this includes sleeping with them. It's important that they can mingle with your energy and align with it: once they have, they will become powerful allies you can consult on a regular basis.

Rune Spreads

There are several ways to divine with runes, and one of those methods is rune spreads, or patterns set out in front of you on a table or surface where each position in the spread represents a significant meaning. These spreads range from basic to intricate, from a single rune to many, and no matter the number of runes in a spread, it's important to keep the intention of your spread in mind. Let's say your intention is that the top rune in a spread represents the past; thus, it will be important to keep that in mind as you position the rest of the runes you've pulled in the spread.

Consulting runes can help you with a crossroads in life where you are having trouble making decisions, such as leaving your job for one that may be better, trying to discern some difficult behaviors in the ones you love, or even getting an idea of what the upcoming day or week will bring for you. Generally speaking, the kind of spread you choose is determined by how much information you're looking for, how complex the situation you're in happens to be, and how much time you have. A one-rune pull is good for a quick question, or a fast way to see how your day will unfold in the morning, whereas an in-depth spread with five or more runes will provide even further insight, such as seeking advice on a new career venture or a possible romantic partner.

Working with runes, either by casting them or setting them out in spreads, is far more than mere "fortune-telling." You are appealing to the greater forces at work in the Universe for insight, and as it is a sacred act in and of itself, it should be treated as such. Working with runes can help increase your intuition and your connection with the Unseen World. In the following sections, you'll discover sample rune spreads like a single-rune spread, the Spread of the Norns, and the Runic River, as well as how to interpret them. Make your way to the Resources section (page 147) to find other books that contain various types of rune spreads.

We should remember that we counsel the runes for their wisdom—they are not dictating our lives. No matter what type of oracle we use, we must always remember that our future is flexible and that we have free will to help us change scenarios. Oracles of any kind, especially the runes, serve us in two ways. The first is to warn us about a scenario about which we can do something, and to advise us to act accordingly so we can do something about it. Think of having a dream about the plane you're taking the next day crashing, and you miss your flight, and it actually crashes. That's one way oracles help us. The other way an oracle helps us is to warn us of situations we cannot do anything about, and to help us wrap our minds around the situation and prepare for it, mentally and emotionally.

We use divination tools like the runes to help us peer through the veil and to gain insight, but we must always remember our free will, and temper our readings with our own intuition.

Remember the practical instructions that come with each rune pull. Center yourself, and settle your thoughts. Whether you do this for yourself or for others, it's important to remember to mix your ond with the runes. Blow into the bag to mix your ond with the runes, chant Odin's name nine times, and then ask your question. Finally, after doing all this, allow Odin, the Norns, and the runes to show you your path forward.

Wyrd Pull—One-Rune Spread

Often times, when looking for a quick, concise answer or guidance to a question, you should pull just a single rune. An example of a one-rune pull would be to find out how your day is going to progress, the overarching theme for the upcoming week, or insight into another person's perspective in a situation. In this instance, when we do this, we call it a Wyrd Pull. This is the simplest rune casting of all, diving quickly into the Well of Wyrd for just a single rune. As with most areas in life, it's best if we keep it simple, and this rune casting does this for us. As we've seen with the runes so far, even when you pull a single rune, you're still gaining access to layers of information and knowledge.

This method of runic divination is a great addition to any morning devotionals, as well as a means to grow your connection to the runes. Honor and invoke Odin, blow into the bag of runes, then ask the runes to show you how the day will unfold, or what lessons the runes will show you over the day. Record that rune in a journal and come back to the journal at the end of the day, recording how you saw the rune manifest itself through your day. This is the best and fastest way to build a relationship with the runes.

Hagalaz

Courtney is using the runes to learn more about the intricacies of the Universe around her, and she uses the Wyrd Pull to ascertain information about a situation in her life. Her husband has been working really long hours and is coming home stressed, more so than he normally is. Courtney has grown so frustrated with the situation, feeling the stress of the husband she loves and thereby finding herself stressed around situations she normally would handle with ease. She turns to the runes for an answer.

Courtney invokes Odin, blows into her bag of runes, shakes them up, and brings forth Hagalaz, the hailstorm, from the bag and places it on the table in front of her. Though many may see this as intimidating, as Hagalaz brings unpleasantness and an upset, just like a hailstorm, there is optimism that comes with this rune. In this case, Hagalaz is a good omen of sorts, as Hagalaz reminds us that no hailstorm lasts forever and the sun eventually comes out. There is a storm over her head, but it will soon pass.

Courtney knows the work situation for her husband won't last either, and Hagalaz reminds her that his stress won't last forever. With the magic of Hagalaz in her life, Courtney acknowledges the storm but knows it will blow over.

Spread of the Norns—Three-Rune Spread

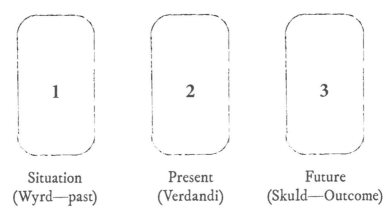

1	2	3
Situation	Present	Future
(Wyrd—past)	(Verdandi)	(Skuld—Outcome)

The Norns are the three weaving women of Norse cosmology, weaving together what has passed, what is passing, and what will most likely pass into the tapestry of our lives. This rune pull gives us a chance to read three runes and offers a deeper look into a situation while not overwhelming us with too much information.

The Norns are a race of beings unto themselves. In the *Völuspá*, the first and best-known poem of the *Poetic Edda* also known as the Prophecy of the Volva (Seeress), we learn of the Norns. The first Norn is Wyrd, or "The Past"; the second is Verdandi, or "What Is Presently Coming into Being"; and the third is Skuld, or "What Shall Be." It is these three that we invoke with this spread and whose counsel we seek.

The first rune you pull will be laid on the left side of the spread, and this represents the situation and what has come to pass to bring the situation into being. The second rune will go to the upper right-hand in the middle of the spread, showing what is presently coming into being, and the final and third rune placed to the right shows us what will most likely come into being and what shall be, should we not divert from our current course of action.

Past   Present   Future

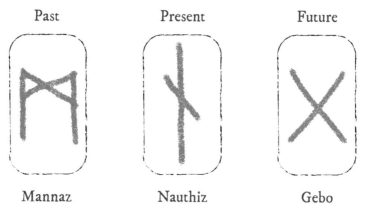

Mannaz   Nauthiz   Gebo

Eric and Aaron have been best friends since grade school, and after graduating high school, decide to become roommates, renting an apartment together. Eric has taken it upon himself to rent the apartment and to take care of the utilities, just asking that Aaron contribute his fair share to the bills. A couple of months ago, Aaron started being late with his portion of rent and utilities. Now, it's been almost a month since he should have paid Eric what he owes him. Eric doesn't know what's going on, as Aaron seems to leave early, and come home late, and he's not responding to any of Eric's messages or emails. Eric is really feeling the pinch, and yet doesn't want to harass Aaron too much, as he's his best friend.

Eric turns to the runes for guidance. Mannaz, the rune of man and the relationships we have with other humans, comes up as the rune for his past. He pulls Nauthiz, the rune of need and restriction, as his present situation, and notes that he does indeed feel constricted and restrained. The present rune is a bit blatant in what it tells him, and yes, the present situation is all about money and resources. Eric is relieved to see Gebo, the rune of the gift and equal exchange, in the future—equal exchange, a balance of sorts that may come about. Nauthiz counsels that we need to dig deep and may have to step into an uncomfortable role to find the balance we need, and Eric is grateful for this advice. Eric now knows what he has to do in this situation: he has to dig deep, find the strength to confront his best friend, and make him understand that it's his responsibility to take care of his half of their shared financial obligations.

The Runic River—Five-Rune Spread

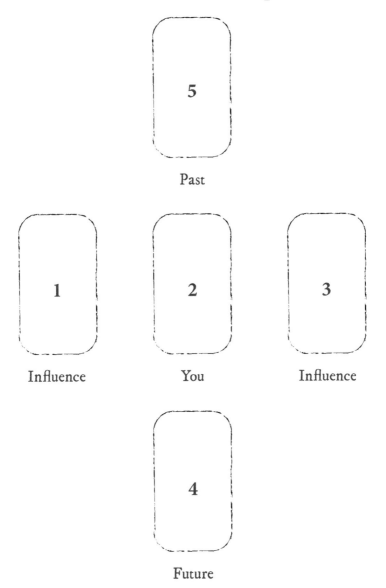

5

Past

1

Influence

2

You

3

Influence

4

Future

The Runic River is a five-rune spread that helps you find a more in-depth look at a situation you're in: what brought you to that scenario, what is coming to bear on the present moment, and what will most likely come about in the future.

This spread imagines you as standing in the middle of a great river. Just like the water of a river has an influence on all parts of the river itself, so does your past and future have an effect on the river of your life. If the water of your river is tainted by unpleasantness, whether in your past, present, or future, it will have an effect on where you're standing at this moment.

The first rune you will pull for this spread is *you*, and you place this in the center of the river. This represents you and the scenario about which you're inquiring. The second rune you pull represents the past, and you place this rune above the rune representing you, or "behind" you in the river. This is the water that has already flowed around you and is now behind you. The third rune you pull represents an influence that's having an effect on your life right now, just like the water beside you in a river would have an effect on you. This rune you pull and put to the left of the rune representing you. The fourth rune is also an influence and goes to the right of you, again representing the "waters" of life that are having an effect on you at this moment. The final rune you pull represents the future of the situation, and you place this below or "in front of" you in the river. This represents that water that has yet to flow around you in the river of your life.

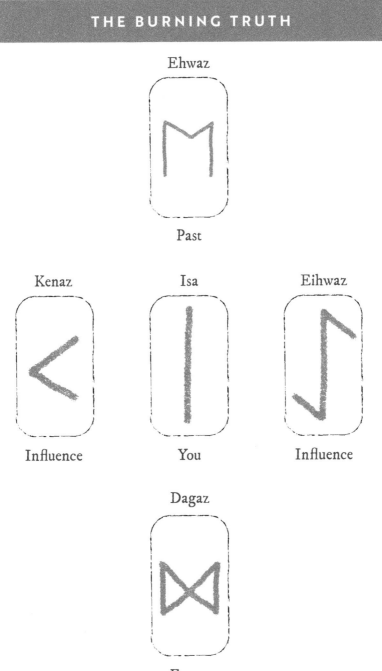

Ehwaz

Past

Kenaz

Influence

Isa

You

Eihwaz

Influence

Dagaz

Future

Jake has had a girlfriend for the past six years, one he hopes to soon ask to marry him. They live together and he feels they are definitely soul mates. In his own secret way, he's already planning for what life will look like after they're married. He's excited about the prospects of their lives together.

Sadly, Jake's girlfriend's mother has recently been diagnosed with breast cancer. This has thrown his girlfriend into a storm of anxiety and depression, as her mom is like a sister— they are best friends. Jake's girlfriend has never really dealt with death or sickness before, and she's grown distant in the process of dealing with her feelings. Jake decides to turn to the runes to find insight into this scenario.

Jake pulls Isa, the ice rune, the rune of stagnation and stillness, as the rune representing himself and the scenario. This represents the coldness he's feeling, but also the isolation he's feeling as his girlfriend seems to be pulling away from him. The rune he pulls for the past, the horse rune Ehwaz, shows that relationships are the root of the issue: the relationship he has with his girlfriend, and the relationship his girlfriend has with her mother. The rune to the left of him is Kenaz, the torch of illumination, representing a "truth that burns," one that has brought enlightenment to both him and his girlfriend. This can also represent the "sore" or "ulcer" that is the mother's breast cancer. To the right is Eihwaz, the 13th rune of death and protection, reminding him that death is around us, that polar opposites exist—what was once happy and pleasant has turned sad and discomforting, both in his relationship with his girlfriend and in her relationship with her mother.

Jake pulls Dagaz, the new day and rune of transformation for the better, as the rune of the future, or of the outcome. This rune reminds him that a change is coming, transformation for the better. He takes hope in this, because there is a great chance for his girlfriend's mother's survival as they caught the cancer early. He sees Dagaz as a sign that the future holds brighter days for all involved.

Other Spreads

There are several other ways you can interpret runes, and several spreads to help you do so. There is a very common spread in runic circles called the World Tree, consisting of nine runes that represent the nine worlds that exist on Yggdrasil. As with the other spreads seen here, we see the positions in the spread as representations of energies that may be surrounding you, and how they're affecting one another. Visit the Resources section (page 147) for more information on other rune spreads and literature, including Paul Rhys Mountfort's *Nordic Runes*.

There is a difference between rune spreads and rune castings. Rune spreads are predetermined positions that represent different parts of a whole—different variables in an equation. In this method, you are taking more of an active role in where the runes end up in the overall reading. With rune casting, however, you are giving up more control and putting more influence in the hands of the Norns. Rune castings are the upending and dumping out of all the runes to see where they land, interpreting them by their position to one another. This method is more for people who are comfortable with reading runes and have built a great relationship with them. After blowing into your bag of runes and mixing your ond with them, you cast them all onto a white cloth, interpreting the runes that have fallen face up and how they interact and influence the runes around them.

CHAPTER FOUR

Runic Magic

The runes are so much more than a writing system, as you've learned from the previous chapter on divination practices. We are shown the various aspects of runology time and time again, both in the ancient lore of the Norse world and from artifacts taken from the archaeological record. The runes of the Elder Futhark offer us a chance to peer deeper into the workings of the Unseen World around us, and with proper usage, we can use them to appeal to the greater energies around us to help us achieve results, in both the Seen and Unseen Worlds.

In this chapter, you will discover the basics of runic magic and how to use the runes to bring about change in your world. It is here that you'll begin to unravel the mysteries of these powerful energies. Remember, everyone comes to the runes from different walks of life and different levels of magical or spiritual practice. You do not need magical or ritual experience to work with the runes as described here. However, even if you are quite adept at magical or spiritual systems, this chapter can be of use to you.

Origins and Practice

The very first myth of the runes comes from the *Poetic Edda*, where we learn of Odin's discovery of the runes. In the *Poetic Edda*, Odin reveals that runes can be used for more than writing, specifically in the art of divination. Although runes have many applications in religious and magical practices, the first and foremost magical use of runes is that of divination.

Odin's journey to the Well of Wyrd and his subsequent discovery of the runes show us that runes are powerful symbols, used to help us divine messages from the Norns and other great powers. We have proof in the *Eddas* and the lore that runes were used for divination, but they were used for so much more than that. There are several stanzas in the *Poetic Edda* concerning the Valkyrie Brynhildr and her advice to the hero Sigurth on how to use runes in a magical way to bring about safety and victory. As we see in the great works of rune scholars like Edred Thorsson, there are archaeological finds like runestones that show us that runes have great power for those who yield them, especially in the use of curses or blessings. Runes have been carved on spearheads, swords, shields, brooches, and even combs.

One of the most famous runestones, called the Björketorp Runestone, can be found in Sweden, standing a mighty 14 feet tall. It forms a circle with two other large stones, and on the stone is a warning, inscribed in the Elder Futhark: "I, master of the runes, conceal here runes of power. Incessantly [plagued by] maleficence, [doomed to] insidious death [is] he who breaks this [monument]." Scholars are unsure if this stone acts as a grave marker or an altar to Odin, or even as a border marker between Sweden and Denmark. There is even a tale regarding a local man who went to remove this stone, wanting to cultivate and till the land of which it was a part. On a day of cool, still weather, this man lit a fire at the base, attempting to heat the stone and cool it with water, thus cracking it into pieces he could remove. As the wood at the base of the stone was lit, a great wind came up and blew the flames toward the man, setting his hair on fire and putting out the fire around the great stone. The man was unable to put the fire out and died what can only be imagined as a horrible death.

There are several ways to bring runes into magical work for you, and around you. The use of runescript is one way, creating an equation of sorts with subsequent runes placed consecutively, just like you would take letters and create a word from them. We can also create bindrunes, a combination of runes, to help us focus the purpose and intent of several runes together.

We can intone runes in the art of Galdr, and we can even inscribe runes on food and consume them that way, bringing the energy and magic of the runes into ourselves.

Principles of Runic Magic

The first basis of bringing runes into magical workings is to make sure that you've built a healthy and stable relationship with the runes. This is done by pulling a rune every day, journaling about the rune, and discovering the energies of the runes and how they manifest in your day-to-day life. To continue your relationship with the runes, it is wise to meditate on them, as well as to make offerings to them.

In this regard, an altar to the runes themselves might be appropriate. Remember, they represent great powers that act as threads in the epic fabric of our existence and they should be respected and revered as such. It is said by some that each rune represents a different wight, or spirit. Regardless of your belief in this, a healthy, sacred attitude toward the runes is necessary to begin working with them magically.

The best source on how to work with the runes magically is the *Eddas* themselves. In the *Poetic* and *Prose Eddas*, we learn of Odin's discovery of the runes upon the World Tree when he sacrificed himself, impaling himself on his great spear. This myth is the basis of all our magical workings with runes; we acknowledge and understand the role of Odin in bringing us the runes, and the sacrifice he made to do so.

This underlying current of sacrifice played such an important role in the discovery of runes, and it should also play an important role in any of the magical or religious ceremonies into which you bring the runes. There are several types of ceremonies with which runes can be incorporated, from the charging and blessing of amulets and talismans, to the appealing of gods and goddesses for a particular outcome in a situation. Whatever your intent, it is always important to make offerings or sacrifices during your rituals and ceremonies.

There are many differences between the magical uses of runes by our ancestors and those adopted in modern times. Edred Thorsson, Freya Aswynn, Ralph Blum, and Diana Paxson have all brought us modern interpretations of runes and their magic. Iceland saw a revival of runic magic in the 1400s in the form of Galdrastafir, the Icelandic Magical Staves, based on gods and goddesses and folklore pertaining to the runes. Guido von List was of great influence on the runic revival and 20th-century neopaganism, giving us the Armanen Futhark, a set of runes he intuited from an 11-month bout with blindness.

Magical practices are covered in this guide, and the following ritual instructions apply to them as well. A basic ritual with runes involves a ceremony in a protected or sanctified space, a circle that's been sanctified as protected or in a building or space that would be considered cleansed and sacred. Before any type of magical workings, it is important to cleanse both yourself and your space, and you can do this in any way that you would like: by smudging, by using flower water or Florida water, or by any other traditional method of spiritual cleansing.

Once cleansed and in your ritual space, you can open a runic ritual by intoning and chanting each rune in a circle. Begin by standing facing the direction of east and chant Fehu. Then, step to the right a little bit, further along the circle and chant Uruz, Thurisaz, Ansuz, and so on. Complete this circle back where you started with Othala (at the end of the Elder Futhark). If you happen to get back to your starting point sooner than you reach Othala, stand there and continue to face east, and chant the rest of the Elder Futhark through to the end. You can imagine the runes as you chant them in any color, but if you're using the runes to cleanse or sanctify a space, imagine them in a great pulsing white color; white is the color of purity, the color of cleansing energy. Our ability us visualize the energies we're working with helps further strengthen the outcome of what we're intending.

After you've called upon the runes in a circle like this, invoke the gods or goddesses you're working with, or any ancestors and spirits that may be involved in the ceremony you're about to perform. Once you've called upon these beings, the work of the ceremony happens. Here is where you would make your offerings or sacrifices, recite your spells or myths, or make prayers and the like that will help you manifest the desired outcome. Once you've completed this part of your ceremony, you can sit in meditation or reverence for as long as you need. Once you've finished, knock upon your altar or stamp your feet three times to draw the ritual to a close.

Runic Talismans

Talismans are objects or charms, usually something you can wear or carry with you, meant to keep misfortune or evil away from you, or to bring good fortune to you, through magical intent.

Talismans, especially those with runes upon them, can take many forms. Usually they are something small enough to carry on us or keep near us most of the time. However, when inscribing runes with magical intent on your vehicles or luggage, perhaps you are in effect making these objects runic talismans. Examples would include making keychains with Raidho, the rune of blessed travel, on them as gifts for your friends and family, or a necklace with Uruz, the rune of strength and vitality, on it to wear in the gym while working out.

You can create talismans with any material, really, yet organic materials work best. Runes are powerful energies that emanate from the Earth and Universe themselves, and it is appropriate to use materials that come from the Earth and nothing synthetic. However, if synthetic materials are all you have access to, they will do in a pinch. Preferably you should be using wood, stone, antler, bone, or leather, and even paper or parchment will do. Talismans can be worn like a necklace or a ring, or they can be something you keep near you, something you place on an altar, or something you gift away.

As we discussed earlier, the principle of sacrifice and offering should be honored here. When you find the material with which you would like to make a talisman, have a small ceremony where you make offerings to the spirit of the material. The Norse ancients believed in animism, in that all parts of the natural world, from stones to rivers to mountains, have spirits, and it is best to appeal to the spirits of the material within your talisman.

Talisman inscriptions can happen in a few different ways. You can carve with an implement, or you can burn into wood and bone using a wood-burning tool. It is often thought important to dye your talisman with your own blood, imbuing the talisman with your very life essence. Remember, if you do this, be safe and sanitary (please see page 34 for tips on drawing blood safely). Never give amulets or talismans with your blood to other people.

In this section, we will cover how to make your own runic talisman, as well as ways to inscribe your talisman. You can draw single runes on a talisman, or you can use runescripts or bindrunes. Runescripts are appropriate for spell work, to bring about protection or defense, love or abundance, whereas bindrunes are great to condense the power of the runes in a small inscription, especially useful when space is limited.

Runescripts

Runescripts are arrangements of runes in a straight line, almost in the way that we would bring together letters to make up words. Runescripts can consist of a single "word" or several groupings of "words," making up sentences of sorts. Once you come up with your runescript, it is traditional to draw a line on both the bottom and top of the word, linking each of the runes together, almost in a box of sorts. Doing this empowers and activates the runescript, tying the power of the runes to one another.

There are several ways you can bring the power of the runes into your talismanic workings through runescripts. These methods range from complicated ways of assigning numerical values based on the runes' positions in the Elder Futhark and running them through equations, assigning the runescripts value in that way. There are also runescripts where people spell out words, translating the word or words of choice from their native language to the Elder Futhark. There are many popular versions of this method to be brought into our life, by translating our names or words like *love* or *hope* into runescripts. There are also runescripts that stand alone, created solely to bring the power of each rune into the "word." Whichever way you use the runes in a script, know that they will still bring the power of that particular rune to the working, so please keep each in mind when constructing your runescript. An example of a powerful runescript would be using your last name, like mine in this example: Simonds (Sowilo - Isa - Mannaz - Othala - Nauthiz - Dagaz - Sowilo).

Runescripts are usually made of three, five, seven, or nine symbols. Traditionally, three runes are used in runescripts for growth and abundance, five for defense and protection, seven for love magic, and nine to help affect destiny, or to change the ripples in the Well of Wyrd. However you make a runescript, whether you're using the runes themselves for their individual power, creating a word translated from its English counterpart, or working some type of complicated equation through it, it is traditional to make something that is symmetrical. If you are translating English words into the Elder Futhark, know that you don't repeat characters if they repeat in their English counterparts. For example, the word *blossom* would be spelled Berkana - Laguz - Othala - Sowilo - Othala - Mannaz.

When choosing your runes, be clear and concise. Do not use runes to excess, cluttering up the runescript with too much power. Once you've chosen your runescript, you'll then choose the material on which you'll inscribe your chosen runes. You can inscribe your runescript on a hard object, like antler or bone, and your talisman will last as long as that material lasts. Or, you can inscribe a runescript on a piece of paper, and it's a very powerful bit of magic to burn that piece of paper to "unlock" and unleash the power of the runescript. You can create runescript spells that can be charged on altars or with stones and crystals, to be saved so you can use them later when necessary.

JEN'S JOURNEY WITH THE RUNES

For this example, we will be watching Jen work runescripts into her life. One possible runescript she can use is that of her name: Jera - Ehwaz - Nauthiz. This is a very basic runescript and one that she can use anywhere, on a necklace, or amulet, or even as a tattoo (though if you decide to tattoo runes on your body, you'll want to have a well-established relationship with the runes, built on respect and reverence). You can see in this short runescript how she brings the power of Jera (cycles, harvest, hard work) into play with Ehwaz (relationships, trust, loyalty) and Nauthiz (the "need fire" that keeps her from being constrained by situations or scenarios that would hold her down).

Jen is also pregnant and would like to incorporate a runescript into her life to help protect her and her baby during the vulnerable months of pregnancy, as well as bring great health. The following runescript goes like this: Thurisaz (left-facing) - Berkana - Ingwaz - Berkana - Thurisaz.

In this runescript, we can see the five runes that would help bring defense and protection to us, but we can also see a beautiful runescript balanced symmetrically. Thurisaz is on the outside of the runescript, pointed out in each direction to help guard against outside forces. On the inside we see Berkana twice, for both fertility and health, and in the center, we see Ingwaz, the great seed, another great omen for fertility and health.

Once Jen has come up with her runescripts, she will then carve or inscribe them on a talisman. Her name would be great on a necklace, whereas the runescript that's meant for health and protection during pregnancy would be great on a belt that she wore regularly.

Bindrunes

Bindrunes are a combination of runes. They are usually two or more runes, laid over one another or combined in an aesthetic fashion. In combining runes in this way, we can accentuate and harness the power of the runes for better effect. According to rune scholars, including Edred Thorsson, bindrunes were very rare in Viking times but were common during the Proto-Norse era, as well as later, during medieval times. Some say that bindrunes are the most effective way to utilize runic magic, and just like any sort of magical workings, it's always best to keep your workings simple and your intention clear and strong. It's believed that a bindrune is more powerful than the individual runes brought together to make it.

Bindrunes can be fashioned in many different ways. The classical version of a bindrune is made with a few runes brought together in a vertical fashion, much like the runes are themselves independently. These types of bindrunes are found historically on weapons, tools, and commemorative runestones, and they're usually meant as protective spells or sigils of tribute. An example of this type of bindrune would be the Bluetooth symbol, combining the Younger Futhark runes of Hagall and Bjarkan, or H. G., the initials of King Harald "Bluetooth" the First, of Denmark. Just like this rune, you can use bindrunes to create a sigil that represents the initials of your name. Another famous bindrune from history is the Gibu Auja bindrune, found in sixth-century Scandinavia, translating to "I Give Luck." This is a simple (thus effective!) combination of Gebo and Ansuz.

Other types of bindrunes include radial bindrunes, the sort seen in the Galdr-staves of Iceland. These are commonly circular in nature, often with runes that appear like spokes in a wheel, or symmetrical in a circular fashion. The most famous bindrunes from Iceland are the Vegvisir and the Helm of Awe. It is said these bindrunes are to be written on the forehead in blood, adding to the idea that these radial types of bindrunes were created for temporary use and worn only when needed. Some of these bindrunes are known from folklore for their purpose of being eaten by carving them into foods prior to consumption, as well as being written in blood on soil. Sometimes these bindrunes were carved on objects and then burned, thereby releasing the spell to do the work intended.

However you create and use your bindrune, understand and respect the power of the runes you are bringing into your creation, and it is with this reverence that you will help manifest your desires into reality.

The image here shows a bindrune I created for a tattoo.

In this bindrune, you will see four different runes brought together to make one. As Freya Aswynn notes, Eihwaz makes a great "spine" upon which to create bindrunes. In using Eihwaz, we acknowledge the protective measures that are brought forth by this rune. As a professional psychic medium, I use this bindrune to help further increase my connection to the Unseen World and the land of the dead.

Seen in this bindrune on top of Eihwaz is that of Tiwaz. This is a rune of strength, justice, protection, karmic balance, and self-sacrifice. This rune is brought into this bindrune to help cultivate the just attitude of a warrior, he who would protect the weak from the strong. Tyr is known as a sky god, a god of war, and this bindrune was incorporated into this rune to help the bearer remain strong in the face of nefarious forces.

The next rune you will see in this bindrune is Ansuz, the rune of Odin. It is a rune of breath, of wisdom, and of communication. This rune is added to this bindrune to help bring in the presence of Odin in all psychic/medium works, as well as to honor the breath with which the author delivers his messages from the beyond. This is also a request to help incorporate the wisdom of Odin in his day-to-day life.

Finally, the fourth rune you will see in this bindrune is Uruz, the rune of the auroch. In all aspects of life, we can only hope to be strong, to be healthy, and to be vital. It is this reason that Uruz was incorporated into this bindrune, to help bring vitality to all workings, both esoteric and mundane.

Creating Your Own Talisman

What You'll Need:

Materials:

- A material upon which to inscribe your runescript or bindrune, such as wood, bone, stone, leather, clay, seashells, paper, or other material
- A natural dyeing medium, such as paint, ink, or blood
- Shellac or clear-coat spray for painted inscriptions
- A leather cord or chain from which to hang your talisman
- Natural items, like crystals or feathers, with which you may want to adorn your talisman
- A prewritten version of your runescript or bindrune for reference

Tools:

- A carving implement, a wood-burning tool, or a Dremel or other brand of rotary tool
- Safety glasses
- A fine, thin paintbrush
- A lancet, alcohol swabs, and bandages, if you're working with blood (see page 34 for safety tips)
- A first aid kit to have on hand

You can create your talisman from any type of material, but as we discussed earlier, an organic material is preferable. You are harnessing the powers of the Earth and the Universe through your talisman, so it's important that it is made of an organic substance, if possible.

For the purposes of these instructions, we will assume that we are using a piece of wood. A softwood like pine or fir is preferable to that of a hardwood, like maple or birch, as it's less likely to split or crack while drying or being worked on. We will be making our talisman with a wooden disc, made from pine, with a hole drilled close to one edge through which to string a cord or chain.

Once you have your material chosen, you'll want to know why you're making your talisman. Are you creating a talisman to attract love? Do you want to protect yourself against evil and nefarious spirits? Will your talisman be meant for healing? Your intention is of utmost importance here, especially for choosing the runes you'll be incorporating into your runescript or bindrune.

With your design in mind, begin carving or burning this sigil into your talisman. You should treat this as a ceremony of sorts, being in a state of reverence for the powers you're invoking. The burning of incense here may be appropriate to help you find a trance-like or semi-meditative state of being. Concentrate on the powers of each individual rune as you carve or burn them into your talisman.

You can now apply dye or blood (if this is a talisman for you) to the grooves of your bindrune or runescript. Once this part is done and it has dried, you may shellac your talisman to seal in the blood or dye. It will be beneficial to incorporate astrological influences into the creation of your talisman. After your talisman is created, you can string it on a chain or cord, and you may adorn it with other natural elements, like stones and feathers.

Now that your talisman is complete, you can charge it! Do so by holding it in your hands and concentrating on bringing your power to bear upon this object, imbuing it with your desired energies. You may also leave it under the full moon or in a crystal grid to charge it.

Other Types of Runic Magic

As you've seen so far, there are many types of runic magic, ranging from divination to the creation of amulets. There are many other types, and there are many resources from around the world that can help you dive deeper into these aspects of runic magic. Find many trusted sources in the Resources section in the back of this book (page 147).

One of the most beloved runic magics is that of Galdr, or chanting or singing of runes. Without formal training, you can create your own version of Galdr by intoning or chanting the sounds of the runes yourself. You can chant or intone a single rune or a series of runes. A great example of this is intoning "Isa" when you are too physically hot, or when you are in a heightened emotional state and you would like to calm the "waters" of your emotions. Chant "Isa" as "EEEEEE-sssssaaaaaaahhh" over and over again, imagining the cooling powers of ice coming into your physical or emotional body.

Another powerful form of runic magic is that of Stadhagaldr, or yoga-like positions that bring the power of runes into your body. These positions are meant to help harness the Earth's powers that run below your feet, bringing them into your body and then into existence. This was developed by the early-20th-century Germanic runemasters.

Runic magic is far more than divination and inscribing on talismans or amulets. You can create and maintain a rune altar, you can meditate with runes, and you can even intone them or ingest them on food. Runic magic can be a solitary practice, or it can be a form of magic to use as a complement to other types of magic.

Whatever form your runic magic takes, please approach it with offerings, as well as the reverence, respect, and gratitude the runes deserve.

PART THREE

Rune Meanings

In this section, we will dive into each of the runes and the three aetts, or partitions, of the Elder Futhark. Each aett is made up of eight individual runes, the first being Freya's Aett, the second being Heimdall's Aett, and the third being Tyr's Aett.

For each rune, we'll go over pronunciation, the phonetic sound of each rune, other names they're known by, and the literal translation. Finally, each rune will be showcased by the keywords you can associate with it. In the subsequent description, you'll learn general information regarding each rune. This is meant to serve as a jumping-off point for your relationship with the runes; as I've said before, your relationship with the runes and what they come to mean to you will be your first and foremost authority.

Within the description of each rune, you'll learn information that is relevant to divination, magical uses of the rune, and parts of the lore that pertain to each rune. The translation of the word *rune* is "mystery," as we've learned before, and the following pages are meant to be quick reference points for you along your journey of discovering the runes.

May the runes—and their mysteries—be with you always.

CHAPTER FIVE

Freya's Aett

The first aett of the Elder Futhark belongs to Freya, the great Vanir goddess of fertility and abundance. Throughout this aett we have eight runes to discover: Fehu, Uruz, Thurisaz, Ansuz, Raidho, Kenaz, Gebo, and Wunjo. This first aett introduces the Elder Futhark and helps us understand some very important aspects of Norse life and what they held important in their cosmological worldview. We find oxen, both domesticated and wild, in the runes of Fehu and Uruz, and the runes of both Thor and Odin in the runes of Thurisaz and Ansuz. In Raidho we discover chariots and movement; in Kenaz we discover fire and illumination. Gebo shows us equal reciprocation, and Wunjo shows us the joy and bliss that come from a life lived well.

FEHU

PRONUNCIATION: "FAY-hoo"

ALSO KNOWN AS: Fuhu, Faihu, Feh, Fe

SOUND: f as in "fee"

TRANSLATION: Cattle

KEYWORDS: Cattle, wealth, abundance, money

||||||||||||||||||||||||||||||||||||||||||||||||||||||||||||||||||||||||||||||

MEANINGS

We're all familiar with the term "cash cow" and that is the energy that Fehu describes. Fehu is the first rune of the Elder Futhark, the first rune of Freya's Aett, and one that marks abundance. Fehu's literal translation is "cattle," and in ancient times, especially before the onset of using gold and silver for currency, there was no more prestigious sign of wealth and abundance than cattle.

Being the first rune of Freya's Aett, this rune corresponds to abundance and prosperity, especially that which comes from the Earth. Cattle, just like all animals, plants, and minerals, spring forth from the Earth, consume that which comes from the Earth for sustenance, and eventually return to the Earth. For millennia, cattle and livestock have provided people with meat, milk, cheese, leather, and more. Having a great herd of cattle in ancient times was a sign of great wealth, and Fehu is a significant indicator of wealth and is a great rune for luck, in general.

This is a rune that signifies attainment of riches and possessions, and can even indicate wealth in forms that move, especially investments. Having wealth was important to ancient pagans, but it was frowned upon to hoard your wealth. They understood that to create more wealth, it had to move, and that it was right and just to make sure your wealth was spread among your family and community. This rune, though being defined as wealth, cautions against greed and warns against wealth only used for personal gain.

No matter our modern concepts of wealth, the ancients thought it good and just to create and gain wealth. Even the Vanir gods and goddesses were deities of abundance and wealth, known for their generosity. Freyr and Freya, twins of the Vanir, were the preeminent god and goddess of fertility and wealth and were appealed to for help with abundant crops, and abundant crops helped create abundant livestock.

Over time, Fehu came to mean money, especially as wealth became defined by gold and silver instead of cattle and livestock. Even those precious minerals, of which still today people are guilty of hoarding too much, come from the Earth. Vikings, the warrior class of the ancient Norse peoples, only wanted enough wealth to start a farm, as having a farm, especially an abundant one, was a sign of great wealth. Again, Fehu is a rune of abundance and, depending on the runes found with it in a casting, could certainly mean that it's time for you to stop hoarding so much.

We cannot create abundance without the act of creation itself, whether hard work, the creation of art, or the tilling of soil. Therefore, Fehu is a fantastic rune for productivity, and for helping generate wealth in general. Be sure to remember that it is a rune that warns against the freezing of wealth, as its energy is that of wealth in motion.

IN MAGIC

Fehu greatly increases productivity and abundance in your life. To bring the energy of Fehu into your life, you can chant it as you are working or acting in any way that helps bring about abundance. Inscribe Fehu in gold ink on the inside of your checkbook or on a slip of paper to tuck away in your wallet or purse, or wherever you keep your money.

FEHU IN RUNELORE

Cows were sacred to Nerthus, the great Earth goddess, and they help remind us that all abundance comes from the Earth. All the foods we eat, every liquid we drink, all that we enjoy comes forth from the Earth and Nerthus herself. She is a goddess of spring and prosperity to whom several Norse pagan tribes paid tribute in hopes of a bountiful season.

Fehu is the first rune of Freya's Aett, so it obviously has a strong connection to this fertility goddess. Freya's brother, Freyr, has a strong connection with livestock as the god of fertility, and one can even imagine that Fehu's profile looks similar to that of a cattle's horns. Use this rune to generate wealth, prosperity, and abundance for yourself, but remember the lesson of Fehu in that money and wealth must move to create more of itself: That which the gods grant us can be taken from us just as easily.

URUZ

PRONUNCIATION: "OO-rooz"

ALSO KNOWN AS: Ur, Urus, Oruiox, Urox

SOUND: *u* as in "usurp"

TRANSLATION: Auroch (wild ox)

KEYWORDS: Ox, health, vitality, strength

‖‖

MEANINGS

Uruz is the rune of the aurochs, a wild ox that roamed Europe, Asia, and North Africa just hundreds of years ago, finally becoming extinct when the last auroch was killed in Poland in 1627. The auroch was the ancestor of domestic cattle, the precursor to the cattle of Fehu.

Uruz is a rune of primal Earth energy. Unlike Fehu, the rune of cattle that comes before Uruz, this is a rune of wild, untamed potential. Uruz represents health, vitality, and endurance, yet it is also a rune of courage and a reminder of how we should appropriately use our aggressive nature. The auroch was renowned for its strength and inability to be tamed, and our ancestors respected them so much they immortalized them in cave paintings found throughout Europe.

This rune is historically interpreted as a very masculine rune, bringing forth a driving force that helps us retain vitality and health, and is great for helping us increase our energy. Imagine the ancient auroch, with almost no natural predators aside from humans, wandering the plains and forests of Eurasia and northern Africa, nearly unstoppable in its prowess. No wonder our ancestors held them in high regard!

Great change can also be foretold by Uruz. This is a rune of creation, and just like the great Audhumla, the cow who nourished Ymir (the first Giant) with her milk, this is a rune of potential. Much springs forth from Uruz, just like milk from a cow's udder. Uruz is a power of creation that dismantles the old and helps bring forth the new. It is a rune of manifestation and helps us find the strength within to bring forth that which we want to create, whether it's a new version of ourselves or something else entirely.

In a reading, this rune could mean that it's time to concentrate on your physical health. Vitality, health, and prowess were respected greatly among the ancient Norse and were no better demonstrated than with Viking culture. "Might is right" could certainly have been their motto, and Uruz helps us to find the might within. Much like the Viking spirit heralds, this rune in a reading could also be telling you that it's time to conserve resources to better consolidate your strength. Finding Uruz in a rune pull or reading could very well also mean that it's time to stop being so "bull-headed" and to stop thrashing around like a "bull in a china shop." Much like the notoriously stubborn Taurus, the energy of Uruz may be telling you to find the courage to step back from a situation and know your own limitations.

There may have been no other animal more renowned for its courageous spirit among the ancient Norse than the auroch, and that's why Uruz is a rune that signifies courage, and not only strength. Strength without the courage to use it, without the drive to manifest it in the right direction, is just like the bull in the china shop we would all do well to avoid becoming.

IN MAGIC

Uruz is a wonderful rune to use when health and vitality are a concern. Drawing it on our bodies in red ink can help intensify our strength, especially before and during an athletic competition or workout. Tracing Uruz on your forehead with your finger can help you find vitality when weak, or awareness when tired.

URUZ IN RUNELORE

Aurochs were well-known and sought after for their horns, which could sometimes reach a span of up to 6 feet. The most well-known drinking vessel of the ancient Norse pagans was that of a horn, and a man would be judged by how much mead he could drink in a single draught. Throughout Europe, drinking horns have been found in the graves of great warriors, signifying great strength and vitality. As the *Prose Edda* tells us, Thor was tricked into drinking from a great horn that held all the seas, and by drinking as much as he could, he created the tides. As part of a drinking contest, this incredible act of drinking scared Utgarda-Loki, a great Giant of Jotunheim, the world of the Giants. Only a person—or god!—of great strength could drink such mighty amounts. This is the power of Uruz.

THURISAZ

PRONUNCIATION: "THOOR-ee-sahz"

ALSO KNOWN AS: Thorn, Thursis, Thurs

SOUND: *th* as in "the"

TRANSLATIONS: Giant, demon/ monster, thorn, Thor

KEYWORDS: Disruption, destruction, protection

MEANINGS

Thurisaz is Thor's rune. This is the rune of the disruptor and the protector. This represents a disruption in the status quo against which you need to be protective. Conversely, it is also the rune that helps you protect. It is the thorn with which you stab and protect yourself, but it is also the thorn that stabs you.

Thurisaz can manifest as a misfortune that takes away the stability in your life, meaning that you may be about to face great challenges and turmoil of some kind. This rune can present itself when you feel like you are being attacked, whether on the physical, emotional, spiritual, or mental plane. Thurisaz shows us that we are being blocked in a way that we may not see immediately, but trust that it will soon show itself to you. In its most basic meaning, you are being opposed by organizations or people that have more "might" than you, and it encourages you to bring about a state of defense, as best you can.

A great analogy for Thurisaz is a hedge of thorny bushes. Imagine standing on the *inside* of the hedge, where you are protected from outside forces. In this sense, Thurisaz is very much a protecting rune. Now imagine being on the *outside* of the hedge and you must get to the other side; in many ways, this represents the thorns with which we must deal in life, no matter how painful they are to us.

This rune is associated with Thor, the Giant Slayer. Giants are terrible, destructive creatures in Norse mythology and, much like a Giant himself, Thor defends the nine worlds against their destruction. Thor is not a god of war, but a god of protection. He swings his mighty hammer, Mjöllnir, to defend Midgard, Asgard, and the other worlds from the destruction of the Giants. In this way, Thurisaz is the Giant from whom we need protecting, but also the hammer with which we protect ourselves.

This rune also encourages us to balance the harsh forces of nature. Thor took on the mantle of Giant Slayer, but it is noted throughout the lore that he doesn't rid the nine worlds of *all* the Giants, only enough to bring balance. This can also indicate that the potent forces of nature must be balanced around you. Thurisaz is one of the most powerful runes in the Elder Futhark, and much like the power of incredible natural forces, it must be balanced.

Thurisaz can also mean a supernatural being of a malevolent nature. This rune can be translated as "giant," "demon," or "monster" and may very well show you that negative spiritual forces are at work around you, especially if it's the result of a divination asking for guidance around opposition. The Giants, or Jotnar, were a race of beings who were both opponents and ancestors of the great Norse gods.

IN MAGIC

Thurisaz must be carefully used magically, for it is one of the most powerful runes. It can be used in conjunction with other runes to help increase the potency of spells or bindrunes. You can draw this rune on your forehead to bring about incredible energy, and you can also draw multiple instances of Thurisaz in rows, pointed outward, to help ward off negative energy.

THURISAZ IN RUNELORE

As the Thunder God of the ancient Norse world, Thor's role was paramount to the lives of the ancient northern Europeans. Thor's physical prowess and strength could almost never be matched, being two-thirds Giant himself, and he carries his hammer, Mjöllnir, almost everywhere he goes. When lightning would dance across the sky, the ancient Norse knew this to be Thor's hammer protecting Midgard from the destructive agents of chaos that were the Jotnar themselves. Before the Christianization of Europe, Thor was revered in cults throughout Scandinavia and northern Europe. He was called upon for comfort, for protection, and to bless people, places, and events. Weddings were blessed using Thor's hammer, so it is a tool that can both destroy and sanctify. You will see Mjöllnir pendants as a very prominent fashion statement today, worn proudly by neo-pagans and Asatru.

ANSUZ

PRONUNCIATION: "AHN-sooz"

ALSO KNOWN AS: Aza, Oss

SOUND: *a* as in "answer"

TRANSLATIONS: A god, mouth

KEYWORDS: Odin, god, communication, wisdom

||||||||||||||||||||||||||||||||||||||||||||||||||||||||||||||||||||||||||||||

MEANINGS

Odin is known as the god of words, poetry, wisdom, and communication, and this is exactly what Ansuz represents. Ansuz is the rune of communication, in general, and the rune of words. It is a rune that is brought forth when we use our powers of speech, when we write poetry, and when we use incantations in spellwork. This is the rune of Odin.

Ansuz is also the rune of air, which is predominantly Odin's domain. Wisdom and knowledge have long been known to equal power, and the ancient Norse valued power under little else. A man who traveled and learned much—as exactly Odin did in the lore—was highly respected, as he was able to bring that knowledge back to his own community. A man with significant amounts of knowledge was a man who could be turned to for advice and teaching.

Ansuz is also the rune of breath, and in the lore Odin was the god who gave spirit and breath to humans. There is no greater skill that will get you further in life than the ability to communicate, and this is exactly what Ansuz portends: communication in all its forms and the great power that comes along with communication. Words are important and should be used carefully, as once they are uttered they are impossible to take back. That is why wisdom is tied to the word in Ansuz—we must be wise with our words, lest we create disaster around ourselves.

Ansuz can be seen in the Old Norse word *anza*, or "to answer" or "to take heed of." Even the English word *answer* can be seen to contain Ansuz. This rune will always have to do with communication, whether by the spoken or written word. When this rune appears, it could very well mean that it is appropriate for you to voice your opinions, to chronicle something from your journey, or to write, as well as represent an encouragement to sing. Consider how important communication could be in your life at the moment, and where it's needed the most. Bring about the wisdom in yourself to communicate wisely and justly, and know the gods appreciate how words and phrases can be strung together beautifully. As Wallace Stevens said, "The poet is the priest of the invisible."

As Ansuz is also connected to the idea of a "god," it can also mean that it's appropriate to investigate the great mysteries further, to increase your knowledge and wisdom in occult areas to bring about greater depth to your life. The appearance of this rune could very well mean that it's time to look to others for that wisdom, as the ancients often turned to Odin for wisdom and knowledge. Know that at all times there is an incredible need for words to be respected and used wisely and that education can only help you become more powerful. Pay careful attention to the way you communicate and how it affects those around you.

IN MAGIC

Ansuz is the rune of breath. You can use Ansuz energy to help you with breathing techniques to bring clarity of mind. Ansuz can also be found in the chants and incantations that bring about states of altered consciousness, thereby helping you find wisdom on the spiritual plane.

ANSUZ IN RUNELORE

As we've discussed already, Odin is the god who brought us the runes themselves, and as we know, *rune* means "mystery." Odin hung over the Well of Wyrd to bring the mystery and power of the runes to us, and as we delve deeper into the mystery that is the runes, we utilize Ansuz energy and honor the Old Man himself. In Norse lore, the Mead of Inspiration or Poetry was highly sought after by Odin, as his pursuit of knowledge was insatiable. This mead would give anyone who drank it the ability to become a scholar or poet, making it one of the most highly sought after prizes in Norse mythology. Odin's connection to the runes shows him to be the champion and keeper of whispered words and mysteries, and we should remember that and honor him every time we cast or pull the runes.

RAIDHO

PRONUNCIATION: "Rah-EED-oh"

ALSO KNOWN AS: Raitho, Raida, Rat, Raeith

SOUND: *r* as in "ride"

TRANSLATIONS: Journey, riding, wheel

KEYWORDS: Travel, mobility, movement, rhythm, journey

||||||||||||||||||||||||||||||||||||||||||||||||||||||||||||||||||||||

MEANINGS

Like so much in the ancient Norse world, Raidho revolves around horses, and particularly transportation by horse. Raidho is the wagon or the chariot that is pulled by a horse and makes for an excellent rune to use on a journey, whether physical or spiritual. Raidho is movement in its most essential: Travel, riding, and movement are all meant by Raidho. It is that which is moved, and the process of moving itself.

After the domestication of the horse, the wheel was one of the first achievements that allowed human beings to traverse great distances and carry great loads. As anyone who has ever traveled by car, train, or bus (or really anything with wheels) knows, there is a rhythm to the movement of the vehicle upon which you travel. This is especially true when riding horses, and learning to ride in the same rhythm in which the horse moves is essential to a comfortable ride. In this way, Raidho pertains to cycles and rhythms, and how the wheel must always turn to right itself.

Raidho may stem from the Gothic *raiht*, meaning "correct or just way to go." This rune can also speak to personal responsibility, of carrying yourself justly in life. It urges you to control and manage your ego as one would manage a horse. Think of riding a horse down a road. You can ride a horse roughly, out of control, and trample over people and places unjustly, just like a person with an out-of-control ego, or you can ride carefully, keeping your horse (re: ego) in check, and minding the well-being of the people and places around you.

The Norse valued movement and action, and it was not in their ways to be still or lethargic. Raidho is a fantastic rune for manifestation and bringing order to chaos in and around your life. Whether you were traveling over the great hills and dales of ancient Nordic Europe or you currently take public transportation to work every day, there has always been a degree of uncertainty and the potential for disaster while traveling. You are away from your home, you are away from your stability, and Raidho helps us secure the favor of the gods, especially when traveling in places unknown. Raidho blesses our journey.

Community was valued by the ancient Norse, and the needs of the community were placed above the needs of the individual. Raidho can also refer to the movement of organizations and how one may move within them. Imagine an ancient cart being pulled before horses in ancient times. Carts, wagons, and chariots were mainly built to carry many people, versus just a single person. This is why Raidho may also refer to negotiations, as we must have the blessings of the gods to move about and manage the ups and downs of trade. Just as a person must come to terms with the horse they ride, so must one come to terms with a person with whom they're negotiating, especially to ensure that the journey of each party is fair and just.

IN MAGIC

Raidho is the blessed journey. Use Raidho when you travel over great distances by inscribing it on your vehicle, luggage, or even yourself. Raidho is a wonderful rune to chant to help bring the blessings of the gods upon you while traveling, and it is an essential rune in shamanic journeying for protection.

RAIDHO IN RUNELORE

Travel was an essential part of Norse life, especially seen throughout the mythology of the time. Freya traveled in a chariot pulled by two cats, Thor rode in a chariot pulled by two goats, and the Aesir gods and Odin traveled the night sky during their great hunts. Having healthy horses to help move people and goods was paramount to the health of their tribes, and these principles were seen even more so in the lore of the ancient Norse. Sunna, the sun, and Mani, the moon, are chased across the sky by two wolves, Hati ("One Who Hates") and Skoll ("One Who Mocks"). When the world ends at Ragnarok, both Hati and Skoll catch up to their prey and devour them, causing the skies to darken and fall. One can now understand why Raidho is so important to the ancient Norse, not only in their day-to-day lives, but also in the cosmos.

KENAZ

PRONUNCIATION: "KAY-nahz"

ALSO KNOWN AS: Ken, Kaun, Chaon

SOUND: *k* as in "kind"

TRANSLATIONS: Torch, ulcer, knowing

KEYWORDS: Torch, burning, knowledge

|||||||||||||||||||||||||||||||||||||||||||||||||||||||||||||||||||||||||||

MEANINGS

As we discovered in the Ansuz rune, knowledge and wisdom were very important to the ancient Norse. What we *didn't* discover in Ansuz, and what is highlighted in the Kenaz rune, is that sometimes knowledge and wisdom burn. This is the energy of Kenaz, the energy of the truth and knowledge that may harm us.

Kenaz is literally translated as "torch" in the Anglo-Saxon Rune Poem, but it is translated as "sore spot," "disease," or "ulcer" in the Icelandic and Norwegian Rune Poems. There seems to be a slight difference between the two, but if we look closely, we can see how they are both connected. Let us remember the phrase, "Ignorance is bliss." When we are no longer ignorant, when we have knowledge or wisdom, we are no longer in bliss. We can see this especially in the journey from blissful child to pained adult. Once we know, we can no longer unknow. Sometimes, the truth hurts.

Kenaz is the rune of enlightenment, especially that of a spiritual kind. It is the rune of illumination and light. Imagine standing in a dark cave, with the shadows of the unknown creeping upon you. In your hand, you carry a great torch to drive back the shadows and illuminate the inside of the cave. You are driving back the unknown, you are driving back ignorance, with this torch. When you have learned of something, like Odin learned of the runes, and then you teach that to another person, you are, in essence, passing the torch.

The fires of a smith in ancient times were highly prized for their ability to craft that which a person or community needs. The forges of the Dwarves in Norse culture were cherished, and many of the gods and heroes of Norse mythology sought weapons and wares created by the Dwarves. In this way, Kenaz is also the rune of craftsmanship and study. When we learn a new subject, when we grow into a new profession, we are burning bright with a fire that allows us to change that which we want. Torches were also very important in ancient rituals and initiations, carried in the hands of both ancient goddesses Selene and Hecate. When one is initiated, they are also brought forth into a new version of themself, much like a phoenix rises from the ashes.

Kenaz is not only the rune of enlightenment, but also the rune of manifestation. You can see the "greater than" symbol of modern mathematics in the rune, but it is also the rune that helps you bring "something" out of "nothing." Know that your thoughts have power, and just like how our energy goes where our attention flows, you can bring about that which you need in life with the power of Kenaz. See how the rune appears as if it grows from a point of nothing to a point of something? This is the spark—the torch—with which you can manifest that which you desire.

IN MAGIC

Use Kenaz when you are studying, or creating, or when you would like to manifest something in your life. You can also use Kenaz when you are in unfamiliar territory, whether figuratively or literally, to help "chase the shadows back." When one thinks of the Law of Attraction, or the manifestation of that which is desired, one must use Kenaz.

KENAZ IN RUNELORE

The Dwarves of Norse mythology live in Svartalfheim, one of the nine worlds upon Yggdrasil, the World Tree. Svartalfheim is where the Dwarves work away, mining and forging great tools and items, and because of this, they were renowned as the most skillful craftspeople and smiths in the nine worlds. They were responsible for forging the long, golden locks of the hair of Sif, Thor's wife; Gungnir, the spear of Odin; and Gleipnir, the binding chain that contains Fenrir. Most notably they also created Thor's hammer, Mjöllnir. These incredibly wise and magically potent beings helped bring about new beginnings, or "illuminations," for many of the Norse gods with their skillful work. They brought forth, or manifested, great items of power using their immense knowledge, and we can see through their powerful works how the energy of Kenaz helped bring these creations into being.

GEBO

PRONUNCIATION: "GHEB-o"

ALSO KNOWN AS: Giba, Gefu

SOUND: *g* as in "gift"

TRANSLATION: Gift

KEYWORDS: Gift, equal exchange, offering

MEANINGS

Gebo marks the seventh rune in the Elder Futhark, and is a likely origin for the well-known adage of "lucky number seven." This is the rune of the gift, not only in the gifts we make but also in the gifts we are given by our ancestors through our genetics and spiritual heritage.

Hospitality and equal exchange were of utmost importance to the ancient Norse. As we saw with the rune of Fehu, it's very important to make sure that money and wealth moves, especially to those who need it, and to those we owe. This is the rune of giving and sharing, and shows us the power of balance in exchange. There may have been no more noble virtue than that of generosity, and again, just like we saw with the Fehu rune, the purpose of money and wealth is not to be hoarded, but to be shared. Those who were smiled upon by the gods had an obligation to return the favor to their tribe and community.

Imagine the life of the ancient Norse, well before any of the modern conveniences we take for granted. When a person or family was required to travel over great distances, there was no such thing as inns or hotels. This meant that the travelers relied on the hospitality and generosity of those whose homes they came across. As it very well could be Odin who knocked on your door, it was very important to show guests privilege and care. When one was given refuge and a place to rest, it was custom to bestow upon their hosts a gift, a token of their gratitude and appreciation. We can also see this in the modern flights of hot-air balloon pilots, when they bring a bottle of champagne along on their trips. When they land in the fields of farmers or landowners, they present the bottle to show their gratitude. This is the essence of the Gebo rune.

Gebo rules esoteric exchanges as well. People believed the gods provided for them, and they also believed the gods took away. This is why there were so many ancient offerings to the fertility gods and goddesses of the Vanir, especially Freyr and Freya. When the gods bestowed favor upon them, they saw it as their obligation to show it in return. Even the great sacrifice of Odin, to himself by himself, upon the World Tree shows us how much he was willing to give up in exchange for the magic and power of the runes.

Gebo reminds us that we also carry gifts within us, gifts that only come from our ancestors. The ancients believed that if you had the ability to help others, you had a moral obligation to do so, and Gebo shows us how important it is to bring our gifts to the world. When you commit to a life of serving others, of bringing your gifts to the world, the Universe and the gods will respond appropriately. This is the essence of luck, after all.

IN MAGIC

Gebo is a wonderful rune to help you increase your overall luck. When used in combination with other runes, especially in a bindrune, Gebo will increase the overall power and positivity of surrounding runes. Much like how "X marks the spot" on a treasure map, to find Gebo, to find the X, brings about great fortune and luck.

GEBO IN RUNELORE

The idea of equal exchange was paramount to the ancient Norse, which can be seen in the use of a hörgr, or the plural, hörgar. Hörgar were a type of altar, constructed of piled stones, upon which sacrifices were made. When the Norse would come upon new lands, they would always build these altars as a way to offer up sacrifices and offerings, most often in blood, to the gods and goddesses they venerated. This is the essence of Gebo, the giving to help balance out the taking. These hörgar were most likely not a primary place of worship, but something that was temporary, most likely utilized by those who were traveling. Hörgar can be found in the *Prose* and *Poetic Edda*, as well as in the Old English epic poem, *Beowulf*. Although blood was prized for its esoteric and metaphysical value, most modern neo-pagans make offerings of wine or mead over their hörgar.

WUNJO

PRONUNCIATION: "WOON-yo"

ALSO KNOWN AS: Wunio, Winja, Huun

SOUND: *w* as in "wonderful"

TRANSLATION: Joy

KEYWORDS: Joy, bliss, peace

||||||||||||||||||||||||||||||||||||||||||||||||||||||||||||||||||||||||||||||

MEANINGS

Wunjo finishes up the first aett of the Elder Futhark. As we can see with the first eight runes of the Elder Futhark, those belonging to Freya's Aett, we have been on a journey of strength and abundance, of giving and sharing. Wunjo is the eighth rune of the Elder Futhark and is the rune of joy and bliss. It shows us what comes about by living by the principles of the seven runes that preceded it.

Wunjo represents joy and bliss, a sublime state of pleasure. This is different than simple happiness. We can be happy in a particular moment. A juicy cheeseburger or a funny movie can make us happy, but joy and bliss are more than simple emotions; they are states of being. It is the long-lasting state of fulfillment that accompanies successful growth and prosperity.

The joy and bliss that comes from Wunjo also comes from giving to your community. Remember the lessons learned in Fehu and in Gebo, the lessons of generosity? This is what comes about from living those principles. Wunjo urges us to always think of the community and tribe of which we are part, and that pleasure shared is pleasure multiplied. Think of the great halls of the ancient Norse. There is a level of joviality and community present, a sense of great abundance and joy by those who share it all around.

Spiritual ecstasy is also a main component of Wunjo. Know that Wunjo is the rune of the happy inner child, the child that lives within you that used to find wonder and joy at the spring of a grasshopper, at the whisper of wind through the trees, and at swimming in a lake on a hot summer day. Sadly, most of us lose the ability to find joy in the simple things in life, and it is very important to strive for a childlike (not childish!) attitude in life. Remember when you were a child, when the simple act of receiving a present on a holiday brought you joy? Hopefully, you were raised in a household that prized giving over receiving, as the ancient Norse would want for you. Not only was the act of receiving a gift something that brought you joy, but the giving would bring you joy as well. If you are a parent, think of the joy on your child's face when they open a gift they've been longing for. Think of the joy and bliss that brings you, to see them happy, to be able to provide for them. That is Wunjo.

When you find Wunjo in a rune reading or casting, know that there is good news on the horizon, or a good outcome to the situation about which you are inquiring. If you are using multiple runes in divination, know that the combination of Wunjo and Fehu readily means that the person in question has a career and makes money in a profession that brings them great joy.

IN MAGIC

Wunjo is also a wishing rune and can be used to invoke happiness. It is a great rune of healing, especially for torments of the spirit or emotion. Draw Wunjo on your forehead to help ease the symptoms of depression, and chant it to help brighten your day.

WUNJO IN RUNELORE

There is much joy to be had in the act of giving, and we can see that in the season of Yule, the ancient precursor to modern Christmas celebrations. Well before the historical accounts of St. Nicholas giving to the poor, there were many Norse stories of Odin flying through the sky on a chariot pulled by the eight-legged flying horse Sleipnir. Notice the correspondence of eight reindeer with the eight legs of Sleipnir! Odin would leave gifts for children in their boots left by the fireplace, and well before our jolly red-clad Santa of modern times, Santa used to be described as a gaunt old man with a great white beard. Think of Odin's associations with Elves and how close Scandinavia is to the Arctic Circle and the North Pole. We can see the Wunjo in the old stories of Odin, as well as with each passing of Christmas and Yule!

CHAPTER SIX

Heimdall's Aett

The second aett of the Elder Futhark is Heimdall's Aett, highlighting the perseverance of the human spirit in the face of adversity. Heimdall is a warrior god, the preeminent guardian of Asgard, and here, these next eight runes show us how we can persevere in the face of adversity, and what comes of that: Hagalaz, Nauthiz, Isa, Jera, Eihwaz, Perthro, Algiz, and Sowilo. This aett shows us how the Universe can bring destruction and restriction upon us and how we can find it within ourselves to break free of such constraints. In Hagalaz, Nauthiz, and Isa, we discover universal forces that would constrain us. Jera is the end of a cycle, whereas Eihwaz and Perthro delve deep into the mysteries of our world, as well as other worlds around us. Algiz gives us protection, and Sowilo shows us the power of the sun, and what victory and success can come from overcoming such adversity.

HAGALAZ

PRONUNCIATION: "HA-ga-lahz"

ALSO KNOWN AS: Hagalas, Hagl, Haal, Hagal

SOUND: *h* as in "hail"

TRANSLATION: Hail

KEYWORDS: Hail, disruption, change, delay

||||||||||||||||||||||||||||||||||||||||||||||||||||||||||||||||||||||

MEANINGS

Hagalaz literally translates to "hail." In the eyes of the Norse, and especially those who relied upon crops for sustenance and survival, there may have been no worse adversary than hail. Hagalaz portends delays and disruptions and should ready you for a potentially difficult time ahead. You are, or will be soon, suffering under a force of nature of which you have no control.

Hail can fall from the sky any time of the year, not just in winter. Just as hail can appear suddenly in a clear sky, this rune portends a very sudden change in your circumstances. This isn't always a pleasant change, either, but one that you will have to bear until it is over.

Imagine your ancestors from thousands and thousands of years ago. It is almost certain that those people from whom you're descended raised crops. As these ancestors of ours had no modern conveniences like grocery stores, doctors, or hospitals, the success of these crops and livestock were the absolute success of their family. There was no other connection to the Earth that was more important than the one that brought us food and sustenance.

Now, imagine being those people when a hailstorm would appear in the sky. They wouldn't have had any sort of modern tools to help cover their crops, and if you've ever borne witness to a hailstorm before, you know the damage hail can cause to plants. Your ancestors, while suffering under the onslaught of hail, would be able to do nothing but put their hands up in the air and plea to the gods to do as little damage as possible.

Hagalaz is that force of nature under which you suffer, but there is a reminder to stay optimistic: No hailstorm can last forever, and the sun always returns. When the sun does indeed return, it will melt the hail that is on the ground, and any crops that remain standing will be nourished by the resulting water. Yes, there is a disruption around you, a force of nature over your head with which you must contend, but Hagalaz reminds you to be strong and to wait for the sun to return. You can see how this melting of ice and the flow of water helps remove blockages, from rivers that thaw in the spring and rush toward the ocean to the tears that spring forth from you as you let emotions flow from you.

This rune reminds us to remain steadfast in the face of adversity, and it is this perseverance that helps us succeed. Each of our ancestors were people who suffered adversity, and you wouldn't be here today, reading this book on runes, if your ancestors didn't conquer, or at least wait out, the hailstorms that rained disruption down upon them. You can make your ancestors proud, and channel their tenacity, while coming to know the power of Hagalaz.

IN MAGIC

Hagalaz is a powerful rune for meditation. Sit with this rune to understand that no matter how bad you have it, you could always have it worse. No matter the amount of crops you have lost, you could always lose more. Chant this rune as you meditate to help find optimism in the most dire of situations.

HAGALAZ IN RUNELORE

Hagalaz is the first rune of Hagal's Aett, the second grouping of eight runes in the Elder Futhark. The first three runes in Hagal's Aett, Hagalaz, Nauthiz, and Isa, speak directly to the perseverance of the human spirit in the face of adversity, and Hagalaz especially reminds us to remain optimistic. In some interpretations, the first three runes of Hagal's Aett are related to the Underworld, and specifically Hella, goddess of the Underworld and daughter of Loki. Hella is sometimes seen as Holda, goddess of the winter, who brought the first snowflakes to the world when she shook out her blanket. The word *hag* comes from the Old Dutch *haegtessa*, meaning "witch." Hags, or witches, were thought to have the power of manipulating the weather and could very well be seen as causing hailstorms and other destructive weather patterns that brought about pestilence and famine.

NAUTHIZ

PRONUNCIATION: "NAW-theez"

ALSO KNOWN AS: Nauth, Nod, Nied

SOUND: *n* as in "need"

TRANSLATION: Need

KEYWORDS: Need, necessity, constraint, restriction

MEANINGS

Nauthiz is another rune in the Elder Futhark that doesn't have many rosy or cheery connotations. As with Hagalaz and Isa, Nauthiz speaks of frustration and hardship. The appearance of Nauthiz in a reading means that you are most likely constrained, or about to be, by a situation or person. This means you'll find yourself, if you haven't already, in a place where it's difficult to maneuver to peace. Suffering is an inherent part of Nauthiz.

Yet not all is lost when this rune appears. Remember, the first three runes in Hagal's Aett speak to the perseverance of the human spirit in the face of adversity. Nauthiz can be translated as "need fire," a difficult concept to describe in English. As it is said, when one door closes, another one opens. Nauthiz reminds us that there is always an opportunity for change when approached properly. This rune also advises us to look outside of ourselves for a different perspective, as we can often be guilty of blowing a situation out of proportion. We are often the creator of our own doom and gloom. Nauthiz can help us battle obsessions and compulsions, and find a better way when it seems like the world is conspiring against us.

Nauthiz is the rune that reminds us of what Plato famously said: "Necessity is the mother of invention." It is in times of crisis, in times of great need, when we frequently find our greatest ability to persevere. Think of the times in your life when you were constrained or restrained by a person or situation. Nauthiz is that energy that lives inside of you, that fire, or "need fire," to create a different and better situation. When most of us have more expenses than we do income, we have a "need fire" within us to better the situation, whether it's to get another job or to better budget our money. As Nietzsche wrote, "What does not kill me makes me stronger."

When this rune appears, remember that the constraints that are around you are opportunities for learning. There's not a single person on this planet who won't suffer from a setback or blockage in life. This is truly the rune that helps us never give up, and find the fire within to make a situation better, or at least persevere while it lasts. When the hailstorm (Hagalaz) is over us, we must find the inner "need fire" (Nauthiz) within us to make the situation better, if we can, and if not, to wait it out until it's over.

This principle is seen in Japanese culture, as well. The Japanese word for "crisis" *kiki* contains two characters, or kanji. The first kanji means "danger," the second means "opportunity." When faced with a difficult situation, we have two choices: The first is to surrender to the situation and to let it overcome us; the second is to fight against it, to find the inner drive and spark to help alleviate the pain of the situation, however we can.

IN MAGIC

Nauthiz can be used magically to help empower other runes, an amplifier of other energies in a runic equation. Nauthiz is the rune of pure will and can be used as such. In a divination or rune reading, the runes that follow or surround Nauthiz are the energies that are most in need of your attention.

NAUTHIZ IN RUNELORE

Nauthiz is the rune of the Norns, the three sisters who weave below the Well of Wyrd, at the base of the World Tree. The Norns are the goddesses who bestow upon children their *orlog*, or fate. All of us have our own orlog, woven by the Norns upon our birth. Although our fates are generally decided for us upon birth, we can appeal to the Norns, very much like the gods do, to affect change. Orlog changes and moves, and there's very little that's woven into the fabric of our lives by the Norns that's absolute. This is why Nauthiz is so important when working with the Norns. Very similarly to the Christianized phrase, "God helps those who help themselves," the Norns will help those who find it within themselves to help themselves.

ISA

PRONUNCIATION: "EE-sa"

ALSO KNOWN AS: Eis, Iss

SOUND: *i* as in "ice"

TRANSLATION: Ice

KEYWORDS: Ice, stasis, frozen, frigidity, solid

||||||||||||||||||||||||||||||||||||||||||||||||||||||||||||||||||||||||||||||||

MEANINGS

As we have learned through Hagalaz, the ancient Norse knew the inherent dangers of ice. That is what Isa represents: ice itself. Instead of the ice that falls from the sky in the form of hail, Isa is the ice that is all around us, springing forth from the Earth. As we look upon the mighty strength of glaciers and icebergs, we can see how ice could almost be considered an element itself, water brought to bear in a most mighty form.

Ice is dangerous. For those of us who live in the Northern Hemisphere, we deal with the potential for ice for much of the year. Ice can be treacherous to walk upon, and we must always be cautious when walking on an icy surface, whether it's ice on the ground or ice on a pond. Ice slows and eventually stops the movement of water, so Isa is the energy of stasis, of stillness. When Isa shows up, something in your life is frozen.

Isa shows us that all things in the natural world can be stopped, or frozen, and indeed it may even be a good thing. We see how the four seasons of nature help bring forth more creation: Many seeds and plants need the cold to help them spring forth. This is why garlic and flowering bulbs like daffodils and tulips are planted in the fall, as they need to freeze before they can grow. All moving forms must stop and slow for a while, lest they risk destruction. A human being can only survive for so long without sleep, as the stillness of sleep is necessary for us to be well and healthy.

When the energy of Isa abounds, it can certainly mean emotional rigidity. As water is very much connected to emotions, think of Isa as the frozen aspect of emotions. It can also very well mean that there is coldness between people, or among organizations. When Isa is present in your life, use the rune that came before it, Nauthiz, to find the fire within you to thaw out the conditions under which you suffer. Know that sometimes we must be frozen before we can spring forth from the soil, a new and better person. The cyclical nature of the natural world can be followed as an example to help us grow into a new and more fully formed version of ourselves.

Though Isa can certainly mean stillness and a blockage of sorts, it can also remind us of the ability of ice to preserve, and to make solid. When Isa appears in a rune reading or divination, look to the other runes around it to get a sense of it. It may seem counterintuitive to see Isa as a good omen for a wedding, but remember how solid ice is, how much it preserves.

Isa also reminds us to stand tall as an individual: It is the literal "I" of the ego. We must be strong in this fiery world, we must be solid, just like ice is. When the world seems too fluid around you, or if your emotions seem to be too much, you can solidify the "water" around you and within you using Isa.

IN MAGIC

Isa is an ideal rune to chant when your life becomes too heated, whether it's physically or emotionally. If your emotional state is too fluid, chant Isa over and over again to bring stillness and solidity to your emotional state. On a hot day, inscribe Isa on your body or chant it to cool yourself.

ISA IN RUNELORE

In Norse mythology, the Universe in which we live was created when ice and fire met. In the beginning, there was Ginnungagap, a gaping voice of darkness and stillness that existed between Muspelheim and Niflheim, two of the nine worlds that exist on Yggdrasil, the World Tree. Muspelheim, home of fire, and Niflheim, home of ice, ignited our Universe when the flames of Muspelheim and the frost of Niflheim met over Ginnungagap. The fire melted the ice and formed Ymir, the first Giant.

Creation continued on as the ice melted away, revealing Audhumla, a great cow. She fed Ymir with her milk and was fed herself by a salt lick in the ice. As Audhumla continued to lick away at the ice, she revealed Buri, first of the Aesir gods. We can see how Isa, or ice, helped bring forth the creation of the world when fire met ice, an essential building block in the creation of the cosmos.

JERA

PRONUNCIATION: "YARE-ah"

ALSO KNOWN AS: Jer, Gaar, Ar

SOUND: *y* as in "year"

TRANSLATION: Year

KEYWORDS: Year, harvest, cycle, boon

‖‖‖

MEANINGS

Jera is the rune of the year. It speaks to good work well done and the harvest we get from said hard work. It is the origin of our modern word *year* and shows us, as the 12th rune of the Elder Futhark, how it coincides with the 12 months of our year.

As we've seen with runes before Jera, like Fehu, and runes after, like Ingwaz, agriculture was paramount to the lives of the ancient Norse of northern Europe. Jera is not only the year but the harvest, that which we reap at the end of the growing cycle. It means "cycle" as well, and as we've seen with Hagalaz, the harvest of agricultural crops literally meant the life or death of the people within Norse communities.

This ripened field is a relief after the trouble Hagalaz, Nauthiz, and Isa can bring into our lives. If we persevere through the hailstorms, if we find the "need fire" within us, and if we can survive the frigidity of ice, we can make it through to a good harvest. This rune means you are blessed with plenty and indicates you should be proud of that for which you've worked. If you are someone who creates, someone who considers themself an artist, or if you've ever built something, Jera is that feeling you get when you stand back, look at what you've created, and feel pride at a job well done. Jera is the bounty you gather when you have worked hard, especially sacrificing part of yourself for the benefit of others.

Again, the Norse valued generosity and hard work, and when there was an abundant crop, that meant there was enough to go around and everyone benefited. Very much like how Raidho speaks to the cycles of the Universe, Jera shows us that we are rewarded for just and right action, for hard work.

It is also a symbol that reminds us of how we should strive for balance in all that we do. To some, the Jera rune appears very similar to the Taijitu, or the symbol of yin and yang. Both show us how we need balance to succeed. As the growing season does best with an opposing cold season, just like we saw with Isa, we are reminded that a healthy bounty is found in balance between action and passivity, between movement and stillness. Summer and winter, night and day, fire and ice—these are all polar opposites that help bring forth the act of creation.

Jera is the rune of cause and effect, i.e., that which goes around comes around. We've all heard the expression, "You reap what you sow," and this is especially true with Jera. If you do not till the soil, plant the seeds, weed the garden, and water the plants to fruition, you will have nothing to show for it. Jera is the reward we're given for effort and work well spent, and by working hard, we help keep the great wheel of the Universe moving.

IN MAGIC

Jera is a rune that works great for creating. Whether you are growing plants in your garden or you're working hard for a promotion, Jera can help manifest your goals. Bring this rune into your workplace or write it on the back of garden stakes. However you use it, remember to work hard alongside the power of Jera!

JERA IN RUNELORE

The benefits of Jera can be seen readily in the tales we learn as children. In Aesop's fable of the ant and the grasshopper, we see how hard work can reward us, and how laziness can be the downfall of us. The ant works hard all summer, harvesting and storing food for the long winter, while the grasshopper lazes about without a care in the world. When winter arrives, the ant is comfortable, living in the energy of Jera, while the grasshopper starves and is told by the ant to dance the winter away.

Though the ancient Norse saw value in hard work, they still revered the fertility gods of the Vanir like Freyr and Freya for bountiful harvests. However, they did not waste the growing season away like the grasshopper, but worked hard for the success, health, and vitality of their families and communities.

EIHWAZ

PRONUNCIATION: "EYE-wahz"

ALSO KNOWN AS: Yr, Eoh, Eihuaz, Aihs

SOUND: *e* as in "eye"

TRANSLATION: Yew tree

KEYWORDS: Yew, death, protection

|||||||||||||||||||||||||||||||||||||||||||||||||||||||||||||||||||||||||||||||||

MEANINGS

Eihwaz is the 13th rune in the Elder Futhark, and it's been speculated that its placement is why many cultures are suspicious and superstitious of the number 13.

Whether that's true or not, Eihwaz is the rune of the yew tree. Out of all the world's trees, the yew may be the most poisonous. The yew tree is seen in many church graveyards throughout Europe, and that's one of the primary reasons it's associated with death. As yew is also an evergreen tree, we can see associations with immortality, because it is "never dying" once winter takes hold upon the landscape. It is also known as one of Earth's longest-living trees.

The wood of the yew tree is known for its flexibility and, in the ancient Norse world, was revered for its utility in bow making. This is one of the main reasons why Eihwaz a fantastic rune for protection, not only because of its poisonous nature and that it would "defend" itself against creatures that would consume it, but also because of its use in the creation of bows.

There is much debate among scholars that Yggdrasil isn't an ash tree, but a yew. Eihwaz makes for a great tool for those who would journey in a shamanic fashion, as well as those who would traverse the nine worlds in trance. As we would protect ourselves when traveling in unfamiliar territories of Midgard, we should also protect ourselves while making our way into other worlds. Use this rune not only to facilitate travel through the nine worlds of Yggdrasil, but to protect yourself while doing so.

Eihwaz is the rune of the shaman or the medium, those people who have one foot in this world and one foot in the other. This rune represents the metaphysical axiom of "As above, so below." It is the rune that embodies the connection between polar opposites: earth and sky, night and day, life and death.

It's a common theme that as soon as we start living, we start dying. This is accurate. Eihwaz is a reminder to us that death is a part of life, not apart from it, no matter how much we'd care to deny that, or whether we have the inclination or ability to traverse realms to experience a reality that isn't Midgard. Death was a constant threat in the lives of the ancient Norse, especially considering that life expectancies were much shorter in ancient times. The ancients didn't shy away from death, though they did their best to avoid it. They knew it was an integral part of life and may even have utilized Eihwaz as a way to acknowledge that fact yet still keep themselves safe from it.

IN MAGIC

The appearance of Eihwaz in divination may mean that death could soon be around you, more than it already is just by being alive.

Use Eihwaz, whether by chanting or inscribing it, to help reach out to the other worlds upon the World Tree. Whether you are simply meditating or stepping into a shamanic trance, inscribe this rune on you to facilitate your journey, as well as to protect you while you're on it.

EIHWAZ IN RUNELORE

Seidr is the art of Norse shamanism, practiced by Vitkis and Volvas (male and female Seidr practitioners, respectively). Often they would travel via trance to Hel, the Norse land of the dead, in search of answers from ancestors. Hel is one of the nine worlds where many of the dead lay, and the goddess Hella rules over this cold, dark place. Hella is described in the lore as having a face of half black, half white, half living, half dead, showcasing the polar opposites found in Eihwaz.

Seidr practitioners would often lead groups of people via trance to these lands, yet it was only the Vitki or Volva that would most often cross through the gates of Hel. Eihwaz is the rune of rebirth and transcendence, and the Seidr worker would forever be changed by their time in Hel, not only through the knowledge they gained on behalf of their tribe or community, but by the experience itself.

PERTHRO

PRONUNCIATION: "PER-throw"

ALSO KNOWN AS: Perth, Peorth, Peordh

SOUND: *p* as in "play"

TRANSLATION: Dice cup

KEYWORDS: Cup, lot, games or gaming, fate, unknown

MEANINGS

Though many rune definitions can seem straightforward, that ends with Perthro. This is the most mysterious of all the runes, and because of that, it is considered by many to be *the* rune of the runes.

One of the definitions of Perthro is "lot cup," and many believe this pertains to games or gaming. The ancient Norse took gaming very seriously and felt that the gods themselves played a hand when the dice were rolled. Perthro can very well pertain to the act of tossing dice or other playing implements out in the act of gaming, and this could have even included runes. Thus, this rune can mean the cup from which the runes are tossed, as well as the dice.

Due to the associations with gaming and play, Perthro is also seen as the rune of fate, destiny, and luck. It is the mystery of mysteries, as the runes are "mysteries" themselves. Just like Nauthiz is a rune of the Norns, so is Perthro. Imagine tossing the dice out in a game of high stakes and hoping or praying for a beneficial outcome. Without knowing it, any hopes and prayers would be an appeal to the Norns, those three weaving women of Norse mythology. There is also a correlation between tossing lots and the actual tossing of runes. The ancient Norse saw runic divination as not only a way to divine the present and future, but also a way to alter the future. By using runes in a magical way, they believed could not only manifest their power in their lives but also "restring" the threads of fate as cast by the Norns.

Another possible translation of Perthro could be "womb" or "vagina." This rune may represent fertility, as well as the womb from which all are born. This relates to the Well of Wyrd. Just as the Well of Wyrd is the birthplace of the runes, so is the womb of the birthgiver filled with amniotic fluid. Just as Odin pulled the runes from the Well of Wyrd as he hung on the World Tree for nine full days, so are we pulled from the womb after nine months. As the Norns determine our fate, or weave our orlog upon birth, there is always a deep, unknowable mystery around what exactly our fate will be.

When Perthro appears, you could soon be on the receiving end of luck, as well as the recipient of something unknown. It also represents creative, fierce feminine energy, as well as spontaneity. Its appearance in a divination could be an encouragement to play more, to lighten up, and to enjoy the fun that life can bring. As we discovered with Wunjo, it's always important to maintain a childlike attitude about life. Perthro could also portend issues you may have with your reproductive system, and may urge healthy choices or actions around such. Because Perthro has a deep association with great mysteries, it could also indicate that you or the person for whom you're reading may have psychic abilities or a propensity to be skilled at occult mysteries. This is especially true when paired with Laguz.

IN MAGIC

Use Perthro to help you increase your connection with the Unseen World, and you can use it in conjunction with Laguz to help increase psychic powers. Use it to increase your luck, or use it with Nauthiz to appeal to the Norns to reweave your orlog, or fate, to your benefit.

PERTHRO IN RUNELORE

Tacitus, the Roman author and historian, wrote of the lot casting practices of the northern Germanic people in the first century CE:

> "For divination and the casting of lots they have the highest regard. Their procedure in casting lots is always the same. They cut off a branch of a nut-bearing tree and slice it into strips; these they mark with different signs and throw them completely at random onto a white cloth. Then . . . looking up at the sky picks up three strips, one at a time, and reads their meaning from the signs previously scored on them."

These lots were most likely rune staves, and we can even see the importance of the life-giving essence behind the runes by their choice of "nut-bearing" wood to use for runes. Using nut- or fruit-bearing wood to make runes is a very traditional method to make your own runes.

ALGIZ

PRONUNCIATION: "AL-geez"

ALSO KNOWN AS: Elhaz, Eolh

SOUND: *z* as in "zebra"

TRANSLATIONS: Elk, elk sedge

KEYWORDS: Protection, defense

MEANINGS

Algiz is the rune of the elk, or the elk sedge. There is no other rune that is more regarded for its protective qualities than Algiz. This rune emulates the quality of the elk: steadfast, protective, and strong. Elk sedge is a swampy plant that elk prefer to eat, and it's a very thorny plant that can hurt you if you don't grasp it properly. There are strong correlations between Algiz and antlers, like those of an elk or deer.

Not only is this a rune of protection, it is a rune that insists we reach out to the Unseen World for help and protection. If you look closely at this rune, it very much looks like a hand, held up in the position of telling someone to "Stop!" This is a rune that is used for protection, but it should also remind you that you are protected—yet be seen as a sign to not be complacent. Remember, the spirit world helps those who help themselves, so don't sit on your laurels expecting your spirit guides, ancestors, and deities to protect you. You are here, in this world now, and it's your foremost responsibility to protect yourself and those you love.

Algiz also encourages us to develop a relationship with our spirit. It is a rune that looks like a person, reaching out with their arms up, appealing to the heavens. This rune helps you connect to ancestors, as well as your fylgja, or the Norse version of your spirit guide. Who would be more protective than your ancestors and your familiar spirit? Algiz encourages us to develop a relationship with our ancestors and fylgja, facilitates that relationship, and reminds us that they are here, protecting us. It also reminds us to root ourselves firmly to the Earth and reach skyward for guidance and protection.

We should remember, when working in spiritual matters, that we must protect ourselves in this world and in the Unseen World; however, we also should know that if we are to suffer a loss or pass through an obstacle, it may very well be for our betterment. Yes, you are protected, but if you must suffer through trial by fire, know that it very well may be part of a bigger plan, one to which you might not be privy. What may be seen as a curse or an infliction of pain might very well turn out to be a blessing later on. Take care of yourself, but trust in your spirit allies and deities to bring you down the path you should be on.

If Algiz appears in a reading, it can mean both that you are protected and that it would be beneficial to reach out to your helping spirits and allies to ask for protection. Be on the lookout throughout the day or in regard to the situation about which you're inquiring. Forewarned is forearmed, but remember to arm yourself in whatever application is appropriate to the situation.

IN MAGIC

Use Algiz as a way to protect yourself, as well as your items, or other people and pets. To keep your pets protected, inscribe this on the reverse side of the tag on their collar. Draw this rune on your forehead to protect yourself when entering into dangerous or unknown situations, and it's a great rune to wear as jewelry.

ALGIZ IN RUNELORE

This rune doesn't exist in the Younger Futhark, so there are no stanzas that pertain to it in the Norwegian and Icelandic Rune Poems. The Anglo-Saxon Rune Poem states:

> *Elk sedge grows in the fen,*
> *Waxing in the water, grimly wounding;*
> *It burns the blood of those*
> *Who would lay hands upon it.*

This Rune Poem reminds us that we shouldn't grasp too hard to those spiritual matters with which we work. Elk sedge can be harvested by those who would be gentle with it, as well as by the elk who prefer to eat it. There are two ways we can go about asking for protection and appealing to helping spirits and ancestors: We can be gentle, asking kindly and with offerings for the help and protection we need, or we can act as a petulant child would, expecting and demanding guidance and protection from that which would harm us.

To which way of asking for help and guidance would you better respond?

SOWILO

PRONUNCIATION: "So-WEE-lo"

ALSO KNOWN AS: Sigel, Sol

SOUND: *s* as in "sun"

TRANSLATION: Sun

KEYWORDS: Victory, power, attack, enlightenment

||||||||||||||||||||||||||||||||||||||||||||||||||||||||||||||||||||||||||

MEANINGS

Sowilo is the rune of the sun. This is the rune of solar light, and thereby lends itself to be a rune of power. For the ancient Norse, as well as many other ancient cultures, there was no power more respected and revered in the Universe than that of the sun. This is the last rune in Hagal's Aett, moving well away from Hagalaz and Isa at the beginning of the aett; this is the rune that melts the ice of discomfort.

Though the Norse saw Sunna (the sun goddess) as warm and feminine, with the heat and warmth she provided, this is a rune of power. The heat of the sun would thaw the ground and cause the crops to grow, as well as provide heat to those standing in its rays. Imagine living in the northern reaches of Europe, close to the Arctic Circle, when the sun wouldn't rise for a complete day after Yule, or the winter solstice. To see the sun come back after an entire day of darkness was the ultimate success: Sunna was coming back to warm their backs, nurture their crops, and chase away the night.

Sowilo is the rune that represents power and attack. This is the will that lives within us all that will bring us to victory. When Sowilo is doubled and superimposed upon itself, it forms the Sun Wheel, a very effective shield. This is the lightning bolt that connects the heavens to the Earth, useful in both attack and defense.

Unfortunately, the Nazis understood and exploited the symbolic power of runes. Among others, most notoriously they used two Sowilos (specifically the Armanen version), with the meaning changed specifically to sieg, German for "victory," as the insignia for their paramilitary forces, the SS, during their drive to push fascist propaganda and to murder millions. Under that insignia, the SS carried out the Nazis' genocidal killing, and sadly, the Sowilo in that form is now and forever associated with that dark and evil time and the Nazis' reprehensible acts against humanity.

Sowilo also represents life force, and links to the powers of the consciousness. As Kenaz is a man-made fire that burns from within, Sowilo is the power of enlightenment that comes from without, raining down upon us in the form of illumination from the gods. With illumination and enlightenment comes power. In the context of our use, this is a positive rune, the source from which all life springs forth on Midgard.

Though the sun is known to warm and bring life, it is also a force with which to contend. It is a destructive force as well, the only force known to the ancients that would melt Isa, or ice and icebergs. This is the rune of invincibility and triumph, and all great triumphs are brought about by one of two great interferences: that of the gods reaching down, like Thor would with Mjöllnir, and blasting obstructions from your path, or by enlightenment and knowledge. Sowilo represents both: the inner fortitude to succeed and bring yourself to victory, as well as the benevolence of our ancestors and deities.

In a rune spread or casting, Sowilo is a wonderful rune to see in conjunction with Hagalaz. It reinforces the fact that the sun will indeed come out once the hailstorm has passed. If found in combination with Dagaz, or the new dawn, there won't be much that will stand in your way.

IN MAGIC

Sowilo is the rune for attack, power, and victory. If you're someone who participates in any sort of competition, Sowilo is a rune that should be important to you. Chanted over and over again, Sowilo can bring about great power, success, and victory.

SOWILO IN RUNELORE

In Norse mythology, Trolls are troublesome and nefarious beings. They are first found in the *Prose Edda*, and are known to be brutish and not especially intelligent. Trolls mostly keep to themselves, staying in caves, swamps, and forests, yet they are known to pester the world of men. In Scandinavian folklore, there are two types of Trolls: the Giants, or Jotnar, and the little folks, or huldrefolk. You already know that the Jotnar are large, quarrelsome creatures that dislike men; whereas they are often confined to Jotunheim, the huldrefolk are found in Midgard.

Whether Trolls were large and brutish, or small and cunning, the power of the sun, or Sowilo, was the only weapon aside from Thor's hammer that could keep them at bay. The boulders that are strewn across the landscape of northern Europe are not there by accident; they are the bodies of Trolls who were caught out in the sun.

CHAPTER SEVEN

Tyr's Aett

The third aett of the Elder Futhark belongs to Tyr, the great sky god of the Norse people, he who is not only a god of war but a god of justice, righteousness, and fairness. Here we discover Tiwaz, Berkana, Ehwaz, Mannaz, Laguz, Ingwaz, Dagaz, and finally Othala. This grouping of runes shows us justice, spiritual growth, enlightenment, and the power of family. In Tiwaz we find the rune of Tyr and justice: in Berkana we discover the birch goddess and her fertility. Ehwaz is the rune of the horse, and Mannaz the rune of human connection. Laguz is the rune of water, and Ingwaz the rune of the seed, and the god Freyr. Dagaz is the dawn, and Othala the rune of family.

TIWAZ

PRONUNCIATION: "TEE-waz"

ALSO KNOWN AS: Tyr, Tew, Tiw

SOUND: *t* as in "Tuesday"

TRANSLATION: Tyr

KEYWORDS: Discipline, duty, responsibility, justice

||||||||||||||||||||||||||||||||||||||||||||||||||||||||||||||||||||||||

MEANINGS

Tiwaz is the rune of Tyr, and we are best to understand Tiwaz by coming to understand the myth of Tyr. There is very little found in Norse mythology or lore regarding Tyr, but one legend that does exist tells us a great deal about this god.

Tyr was the sky god of the ancient Norse, and many scholars claim he was worshipped well before Odin, with more reverence. The name of Tyr stems from the Indo-European Dyaus, or Deiwos, which later branched off to include the well-known Greek god, Zeus. Tyr was one of the primary war gods of the Norse, alongside Odin and Thor, yet he is much more than simply a war god. He is a god of justice and law, of spiritual balance and rightness.

The most well-known tale of Tyr is the Binding of Fenrir, or Loki's brother, the wolf. Fenrir was a wolf pup that was growing at a rapid rate, so quickly the gods feared for their safety. The gods entreated the Dwarves to make chains for Fenrir with which to bind him, so he couldn't escape and be a threat. Fenrir, ever suspicious, would only wear the chains the gods brought to him if a god would put their hand in his mouth as a sign of good faith. Tyr was the only god to step up to the challenge, and when Fenrir was incapable of breaking free of the chains that bound him, he bit off Tyr's hand.

Tiwaz is the rune of cosmic order, especially justice as decided by war. The Norse were honorable, as much as they could be, in their pursuit of war, and oftentimes the day and times of battles were decided beforehand. Also, it was custom that war could be averted by a duel, letting the gods decide the fate of the two warring parties by whom they designated the winner. Tiwaz, much like a spear itself, has been found in archaeological records etched and carved into spears and other weapons.

This is the rune of the spiritual warrior, urging us to pay close attention to honor, integrity, and duty, and it calls us to selflessly serve a higher power, through self-sacrifice if necessary. Tiwaz can lend moral strength to those who need it, providing the will to succeed and, when used in combination with Sowilo, provides almost unstoppable force. Tiwaz reminds us of the importance of upholding promises and oaths, and that all of our actions should be rooted in principle. We must be courageous in the face of adversity, tenacious in our pursuit of fairness, and disciplined in how we carry ourselves.

When Tiwaz appears in a rune spread or casting, it can indicate the need to be right, just, and strong. Look out for legal problems or situations in which you must stand up for yourself or others. If you are not in a situation currently where you will need to seek justice, you soon will be. Harness the power of Tiwaz to help see you through.

IN MAGIC

Tiwaz can be used in any sort of combat situation, whether you practice martial arts or are heading to court in a legal situation. Invoke Tiwaz to help you find victory in any sort of conflict. Chant this rune before entering into conflicts, or inscribe it on any tools you might bring to a competition.

TIWAZ IN RUNELORE

There are parallels between the loss of Tyr's hand and the loss of Odin's eye. Odin lost his eye in the pursuit of wisdom; Tyr lost his hand to make sure that wisdom wasn't lost to the destruction of Fenrir. In fact, Fenrir is supposed to finally break free during Ragnarok, consuming all within his path and eventually killing Odin. The gods saw the potential for Fenrir to wreak havoc across the nine worlds, so it was of utmost importance to restrain him for as long as they were able.

Both of these losses speak to self-sacrifice as a way to procure order, and to duty toward others and a commitment to a higher power. One can also see how important honor and law was in regard to war, as warriors who fought bravely and with honor found themselves in Odin's great hall in Asgard known as Valhalla.

BERKANA

PRONUNCIATION: "BER-kahn-ah"

ALSO KNOWN AS: Bjorken, Beorc, Brica

SOUND: *b* as in "birch"

TRANSLATION: Birch tree

KEYWORDS: Birch tree, fertility, beginnings, healing

MEANINGS

Berkana, simply put, is the rune of the birch tree, or of the Birch Goddess, Bercha or Bertha. It's also the rune of birth, and fertility, and was sacred to the Norse people for many reasons. Berkana represents the ripe fertility of the field and, traditionally, the fertility of female beings of all sorts, humans included. (However, this doesn't preclude it from being symbolically relevant to people who aren't women; rather, it represents nurturing and caring in all its forms, for people of all genders.)

When looking at Berkana, many believe it represents swollen breasts during pregnancy. Berkana is sometimes called the "Mother" or the birth rune. It signifies passage and birth, whether a physical birth into our world, or the birth of an idea. Berkana also protects and guides parents and children, often as a mother herself would.

There are two aspects to Berkana, though; not only is it a rune of birth, it's a rune of *rebirth*. It signified the great cycle of life, death, and rebirth. Indeed, when one cuts a birch down, it will almost always spring back to life from the stump with seedlings. This is a great rune of healing, regeneration, and new growth, especially that which comes from old roots. Every ending is a new beginning, as we often hear. With that being said, Berkana is also a reminder to us that we must clear away the old before beginning anew.

Berkana is also a rune of becoming. No birth, whether physical or figurative, has come about without the force of itself, coming into being. Yes, although outside influences are certainly at play, no one and nothing comes into existence without the sheer force of itself coming to bear. A baby is born when a baby is ready to be born, and we can only hope the birthgiver is ready as well.

Berkana is known as a healing rune because the birch tree has many healing aspects to it. Oil made from birch, as well as a tea made from the leaves, can be used to heal, as well as to calm. The chaga mushroom, known only to grow on the birch tree, is the world's most potent antioxidant superfood, and just like ginseng in times gone past, is at risk of becoming overharvested by those who know of its incredible healing abilities.

When pulled in a drawing, Berkana doesn't always mean an actual, physical birth. It will, however, always guarantee the start of something new. Whichever way Berkana plays into your rune drawing, be sure that you're ready for a new beginning, and be sure that you're ready to clear away the old to make way for the new.

IN MAGIC

Berkana is a great rune to use magically, both in actual fertility and in any new projects. For prospective parents who are having a hard time conceiving, this rune is useful to draw on the stomach of the birthgiver. You can also draw the rune in the air with your finger or a wand, chanting or intoning the rune while imagining the beginning of that which you desire.

BERKANA IN RUNELORE

Birches—and thus the Berkana rune—have always been known to have purification and healing properties. There are many rites and rituals in ancient Norse cultures around the birch tree. Birch branches and leaves were boiled, both as tea, but also as a cleansing water of sorts, used to sprinkle or soak items and people to drive away and repel evil spirits. A "birching" (whipping with birch branches) was one of the folk rites of Holland, used to whip women for fertility, and bundles of birch twigs were tied to the door of newlyweds. Brooms were made of birch to drive away evil spirits, and boughs of birch were hung over the doors of homes for good luck. It was known to be the main wood for fires during Beltane, and oftentimes maypoles were made from birch. It also plays a significant role in other northern European cultures; for example, it is the first letter in the Irish alphabet, the ogham.

EHWAZ

PRONUNCIATION: "EH-waz"

ALSO KNOWN AS: Eh, Exauz, Eyz

SOUND: *e* as in "equal"

TRANSLATION: Horse

KEYWORDS: Partnership, trust, loyalty, cooperation, motion

MEANINGS

Ehwaz is the rune of the horse. It is the rune of partnership, cooperation, trust, and loyalty. This rune represents working in tandem, symbolized by the relationship of the horse and rider. It is a symbol of symbiosis, of two separate entities coming together and hopefully creating a union that's more beneficial to both, preferable to an existence of isolation and working by oneself to make it through the world.

Partnerships are relationships that should serve both parties equally, and any partnerships that benefit only one side are not truly partnerships, but relationships where one party gives up more of itself to the benefit of the other party. If you've ever worked with horses, you know that they are to be respected and treated with care; you know that a truly proper relationship with a horse is one of partnership, not of dominance. If you've never worked with horses, you can still see this principle—or lack of principle—in the relationships around you.

Imagine a horse and rider coming together. If the relationship is one of mutual respect, then both the horse and rider find themselves at their destination faster and with more precision than if they were on their own. Now, if the horse doesn't respond to the rider or the rider abuses the horse, the principle of Ehwaz is out of balance and needs to be addressed; in this instance, the horse and rider should never have come together in the first place. Together, with mutual respect, the horse and rider are stronger.

Ehwaz reminds us about boundaries, of where they are drawn, and how we should be clear in setting our limits. This principle of right relation is seen in the Gebo rune, of equal exchange. Those who bring Ehwaz energy into their lives are bringing the energy of Gebo and equal exchange into their lives as well. If there is a lack of equanimity, there is a lack of right relationship.

This idea of right relationship and balance between two parties applies to the relationship we have with ourselves. Not only can you ride others too hard, but you can ride yourself too hard, as well. This rune reminds us to not allow ourselves to be ridden by those around us, whether friends, family, loved ones, coworkers, or professional acquaintances, but also to not ride ourselves too hard. Life is much easier when we become our own best friend, rather than our own worst enemy.

Ehwaz also indicates motion and change. Just like the motion of a horse underneath us, galloping across the landscape, change happens to us and around us as we traverse our lives. Not only is Ehwaz (the horse) closely tied to Raidho (the chariot), but it also reinforces the idea of a journey over unknown terrain. When we enter into partnerships of any fashion, change is inevitable. To make the most of it, respect those around you with whom you enter into partnerships.

IN MAGIC

Ehwaz is a useful rune to use when journeying to other worlds on Yggdrasil. It's beneficial for trancework, journey work, and altered states of consciousness. You can also chant or inscribe Ehwaz to reinforce partnerships into which you enter, whether they are romantic, platonic, legal, or professional.

EHWAZ IN RUNELORE

The idea of the fylgja (pronounced "FILG-ya") runs deep through Norse mythology and spirituality. The fylgja is translated as "follower" and is a helper spirit, generally going forth before the person to whom they are connected. Most often the fylgja is an animal, but it's been noted that a person's fylgja can be a person. The idea of a spirit familiar, found in the folktales of European witches and sorcerers, can very well be seen as that of a fylgja.

One of the most famous fylgja in Norse mythology is Sleipnir, Odin's eight-legged horse. Sleipnir is one of Odin's many helping spirits, which also include the two ravens Huginn and Muninn ("Thought" and "Memory"). Sleipnir is a child of Loki, who became pregnant by a stallion after shapeshifting into a mare. Sleipnir helps Odin travel between the nine worlds of Yggdrasil. You can imagine that Odin, with his eminent wisdom and knowledge, treats Sleipnir with much respect.

MANNAZ

PRONUNCIATION: "MAN-naz"

ALSO KNOWN AS: Man, Manna, Mathr

SOUND: *m* as in "man"

TRANSLATIONS: Man, mankind

KEYWORDS: Man, humanity

|||||||||||||||||||||||||||||||||||||||||||||||||||||||||||||||||||||||||||

MEANINGS

Mannaz is the rune of man, humanity, and mankind. Named after Mannaz, the "father of the Teutonic peoples," this rune is sometimes connected with Heimdall, a member of the Aesir and foremost guardian of Asgard, also known as the "Father of Men." This is the rune of the self, yet also the rune of all humankind, and it represents how our relationship with ourselves is reflected in relationships with others.

This is the rune of the human condition, and how it applies to ourselves and those around us. Mannaz rules the human potential, and shows us that our relationship to one another is of incredible importance to us. We are less powerful, less connected, when we lack community and connection to others. This is man in both the singular and plural sense—how a person interacts with their fellow man is key to human survival and our ability to thrive.

When you gaze upon Mannaz, it appears as if two people are standing face-to-face, with their hands on each other's hips. This is the rune of interdependence, and of the gifts we bring to bear upon our fellow humans via community. Your talents and abilities, or gifts as seen in Gebo, are what give you value to those around you, and it is very important to share those talents and gifts with others.

Mannaz can often relate to friendships, romantic relationships, or partnerships, much in the way that Ehwaz does (and, in fact, you can see Ehwaz as a base of Mannaz). We must strive to treat our fellow man with respect, but we must also strive to treat ourselves with respect. Whether we know it or not, we are attached to those around us, in both a literal and figurative sense. In the study of metaphysics, there is a notion that we create "cords," or etheric attachments, to other people, and this is what Mannaz represents. Using the principles of Gebo and Ehwaz, of equal exchange and right relations, will help us keep the energy of Mannaz balanced around and within us. Mannaz also shows us how important it is to be self-centered, but not in a selfish way. We must take care of ourselves before we take care of others. Self-care is not selfish, and is, in fact, the best way to value those around us. This is the essence of Mannaz.

Much in the same way that the Norse valued wealth, as seen in Fehu, it was honorable to accrue much wealth so that wealth could be given to others, passed along to the community. Wealth must move back into the community, must constantly be moving, to create more of it. The ancient Norse valued their ability to give, but only if they had enough to give, and this is why they strived so much to accumulate more—it was important to be able to give more to those around oneself. We take care of others by taking care of ourselves, and we take care of ourselves by taking care of others.

IN MAGIC

Use Mannaz to cultivate more of your own potential. There is something deeply and inherently human in each of us, and the world benefits by sharing that with others. Whether it's creative pursuits, professional aspirations, or simply a way to live to your highest potential, invoke Mannaz to help bring forth that from which the world—and you—will benefit.

MANNAZ IN RUNELORE

We see the idealization of the self highly valued in Norse culture. The sagas and songs of great heroes and warriors show us how the ancient Norse idealized self-actualization. Conversely, it was also very important to take care of one's family and community.

As we read in the *Hávamál*:

> *Wealth will pass,*
> *Men will pass,*
> *You too, likewise, will pass.*
> *One thing alone*
> *Will never pass:*
> *The fame of one who has earned it.*

The great kings, warriors, and deities of Norse culture were incredibly strong individuals, but they never operated outside of the matrix of their communities. The gods found renown, much like the great people of the Norse culture, but none of their great deeds were done by or for themselves. The benefits always rippled out into the larger community, and the more a person affected great change within the community, the more they were remembered for it.

LAGUZ

PRONUNCIATION: "LAH-gooz"

ALSO KNOWN AS: Lagus, Laaz, Lago, Logr

SOUND: *l* as in "lagoon"

TRANSLATIONS: Lake, water, ocean

KEYWORDS: Water, sea, lake, ocean, intuition

MEANINGS

Water is life, it's been said, and that's certainly what Laguz represents: water, and all the life-giving abundance it represents. In the ancient Norse world, travel was often over waterways, whether rivers, lakes, or oceans, and people understood how much water was necessary for life itself. When this rune is drawn, especially with Raidho or Mannaz, it can often mean a literal journey over a body of water.

Water is everywhere—in us, in the ground below us, and in the sky above us. Water sustains, and water moves. To better understand the wonder of Laguz, we have to acknowledge both the physical water in our world around us, and the metaphorical water of our psyche. Laguz represents the ebb and flow of our unconscious, our emotional state. Emotions are typically associated with water, and our emotions are mainly part of our subconscious realm. We all have hidden springs within us, and Laguz helps us discover them, whether in our waking state or our dreaming state.

Whenever we experience heavy emotions, it often feels like we're "drowning." Many people who are overemotional often refer to themselves as "watery," and indeed, tears are the water that springs forth from us when we are experiencing emotions that are too much for us in the moment, whether they're tears of happiness or tears of sadness. There are many expressions about water around emotions, like "Go with the flow" or "Keep your head above water." The connections between water and emotions have been with us since time immemorial.

Water is also one of the main four elements, the others being earth, air, and fire. Just like these other elements, water cannot be controlled easily by humans, and if in enough quantity and force, it can never be controlled. Laguz represents the basis of organic life, for without water life couldn't exist. It also represents the passage between life and death—one must cross the river Gjöll in order to reach Hel, the Norse realm of the dead.

As water is one of the elemental forces of our world, and can also be considered the lifeblood of our Mother Earth, water and Laguz have feminine correlations as well. This association is further strengthened by the legend of Nerthus, the great Norse goddess of the Ocean. As we are mainly creatures of water, so is the Earth beneath our feet. Thus, Laguz can be interpreted as the rune of the goddess Nerthus, who had a temple on an island in the ocean, and to whom the ancient Norse appealed for safe passage over the ocean.

Laguz is the rune of psychic powers and intuition, as well. When you see Laguz in a reading, it can very well mean that you should trust your intuition, or that there's a need to further develop it.

IN MAGIC

You can use Laguz to help further develop your own intuition, as well as to help ease emotions. You can draw Laguz on your forehead with your finger, as well as intone the rune while doing so, to help increase those powers. Laguz is a great rune for creativity, and can be used in the same way to help with writer's block. Laguz helps heal emotions, and much like Berkana, can be used to help heal the reproductive system, as well as to ease the discomfort of menstruation.

LAGUZ IN RUNELORE

Laguz represents the primal cosmic water that springs forth from Niflheim, energized by the fires of Muspelheim. Thereby, as the Norse world was created by "ice and fire," Laguz is seen as the greatest transporter and carrier of life.

Water—and Laguz—was seen almost everywhere in Norse life and mythology. The Well of Wyrd sits beneath Yggdrasil, the World Tree, and feeds it. The runes themselves sprang forth from this well, ultimately birthing themselves from a watery womb, as we all do. As we all come from water, we also all return to water—a person cannot get to Hel, the realm of the dead, without crossing over the river Gjöll.

INGWAZ

PRONUNCIATION: "ING-waz"

ALSO KNOWN AS: Inguz, Enguz

SOUND: *ng* as in "ringing"

TRANSLATIONS: Ing, Freyr

KEYWORDS: Freyr, male, masculinity, seed, sexuality, fertility, ancestry

||||||||||||||||||||||||||||||||||||||||||||||||||||||||||||||||||||||||||||

MEANINGS

Ingwaz is the great seed, the rune of Freyr. Freyr, twin brother to Freya, is a god of the Vanir tribe, appealed to by the ancient Norse for abundant crops and prosperity. Ingwaz historically represents the masculine energy found in the cosmos and is cherished as a great rune of fertility.

Statues have been found of Freyr with a great phallus, so it is very easy to make the assumption that Freyr was a fertility god. Ingwaz represents this very principle, one of sexuality, fertility, and expansive growth. As one can see from the very shape of the rune, it appears very much like a seed, or even a DNA helix. Interestingly, Ingwaz may be considered the counterpart of the fertile Berkana rune, and the two runes could possibly "slide" into one another, creating a union.

Ingwaz represents the ancestral line as well, the one that comes down through bloodlines. It is the great seed that gets passed down to us, and the one that we pass along to future generations. To the Norse, we were all products of our family and ancestors, and our descendants were products of us and our lives. This is especially seen in the concept of orlog, a type of fate that is a person's luck of sorts, but also that of a family. As described previously, the Norns are said to weave a person's orlog when they are born, and though it's new to each individual, it is also woven from the threads that have come before us from our ancestors.

This is a fertile, empowering rune. Just like Berkana can be said to represent the feminine and mothers, so can Ingwaz be said to represent the masculine and fathers. Although there are no significant myths regarding Freyr, we know from references in the lore that he is a grain god. Grain is grown and harvested, and then the seeds are planted to ensure the continual growth of grain. In this way, we can see Ingwaz as the seed that is passed from generation to generation to ensure the successful continuation of a family line.

Ingwaz is also named after Ing, or Yngvi, a great god known by some to be another name for Freyr. Ing came to be known as an ancestral god, or the Great Ancestor, with many tribes throughout northern Europe being named for him. Some even claim that there is a correlation between Ing and the Angles, for which England has been named, one of the Germanic tribes that settled in England in the Middle Ages. Yngvi could even be Freyr's true name. Yngvi is known in Norse mythology as the source of the Yngling family line, a legendary dynasty of kings from Sweden, from which the earliest Norwegian kings were said to be descended.

IN MAGIC

Ingwaz can be used to help with matters of sexuality and potency. Just like Jera and Fehu, it can be employed with great success in gardening endeavors, as well as those that involve creativity. Because of the association with grain, invoke Ingwaz for matters concerning bread, baking, and even the brewing of beer.

INGWAZ IN RUNELORE

Ing, or Freyr, was known for his prosperity, well-being, and fertility wherever he was worshipped, in whatever form he was worshipped, all throughout northern Europe. Freyr's home is Alfheim, home of the Elves, and Freyr is known by many as the King of the Elves. In the lore, Elves are beautiful beings, feared and respected by all, divided into two groups: the Light Elves, who lived above ground or in Alfheim, and the Dark Elves, who lived underground, much like the Dwarves. Associated with the Earth, both Light and Dark Elves were seen as minor gods of fertility and nature, revered for their abundance-giving or -taking powers, just like Freyr. Elves were known to cause humans to fall ill, but were also able to cure humans with their magical abilities. Even now, in modern-day Iceland, people respect and revere the Elves, building roads and structures around natural features thought to be inhabited by them.

DAGAZ

PRONUNCIATION: "DAH-gaz"

ALSO KNOWN AS: Dags, Daaz, Dag, Daeg

SOUND: *d* as in "day"

TRANSLATION: Daybreak

KEYWORDS: Day, dawn, transformation, balance

||||||||||||||||||||||||||||||||||||||||||||||||||||||||||||||||||||||||||

MEANINGS

Dagaz is the rune of the day and daybreak. It is the rune of the dawn, of night succumbing to day, of the balancing of two points. It is a rune of great transformation, of a new day. Much like Sowilo is the rune of the sun, Dagaz is the rune of the day that Sowilo brings us.

The ancient Norse kept calendars by the moon, and daylight always meant the end of one cycle and the beginning of another. This was especially true for the winter solstice, when many parts of the northern reaches of Europe would see a complete day of darkness. As Jera, the 12th rune, marks the summer solstice, Dagaz is the rune that marks the winter solstice, the coming light that is welcomed after the first day of winter.

Dagaz is a very positive rune, meaning that great things are coming your way. Imagine yourself on a long trek through a terribly long night. Throughout all of human history, the night has been feared, as well as the creatures that dwell within it. On your journey, you crest a hill and overlook a great valley, and then the sun peaks above the mountaintops to the east. You celebrate the new day as the night is chased away, along with the beasts that dwell within it. This is the liminal space that exists between two polar opposites, and it promises the light that comes at the end of the tunnel.

Dagaz also represents spiritual enlightenment, very much in the way Kenaz does. Instead of the burning that is associated with the "harsh truths" of Kenaz, Dagaz is the space represented by the bridging of two opposites of our internal landscapes. We are all made up of intuitive and rational pieces, and only when we bridge those two parts of ourselves together will we know our true potential. Dagaz is the blending of the analytical and emotional, the intuitive and rational parts of our brain. Rather than the quick lighting of the torch that is Kenaz, Dagaz is the gradual, and even slow at times, dawning of a new light that helps illuminate that which is in darkness.

Dagaz also indicates a slow progression of change, rather than the burning intensity of Kenaz or the bright sudden power of Sowilo. As the Earth tilts slowly on its axis and the sun slowly makes its way across the horizon as the year progresses, this rune reminds us that better times and positive change comes one day at a time.

When this rune appears in a reading, know that better times are ahead. In a rune casting or spread, this is a wonderful rune to appear alongside Hagalaz. As Hagalaz is the hailstorm, the catastrophe over our heads of a natural variety, we are promised the daylight and the new day when Dagaz appears. No matter how hard the hail is falling on our heads in the current moment, we must know that better times are ahead. This rune helps us maintain a positive attitude and persevere in the face of adversity.

IN MAGIC

Dagaz is a wonderful rune to use when opening or closing a ritual or magical working of any type, or creative project for that matter. It is a rune that helps bring about transformation and one that is great for helping us transition, whether physically or emotionally, into a better space.

DAGAZ IN RUNELORE

The god Balder is a member of the Aesir, son of Odin and Frigg. Known for his features, he is so handsome that he radiates light. He is loved by all the gods, unable to be scathed by weapons of any kind because his mother Frigg received oaths from everything in the world to not harm Balder. But she forgot mistletoe, which the great trickster Loki fashioned into a spear, giving it to Balder's brother, Hoder, who then threw it at Balder, spearing him and killing him.

Balder's death brings about Ragnarok, the destruction of the nine worlds. No matter the desolation that Ragnarok brings upon the nine worlds, after three, long sunless winters, Balder is resurrected and comes back as the great dawn, shining light upon the world. In this myth we see the power of Dagaz; we see that no matter how dark the night, daylight always returns.

OTHALA

PRONUNCIATION: "OH-tha-la"

ALSO KNOWN AS: Othila, Odil

SOUND: *o* as in "oval"

TRANSLATIONS: Inheritance, legacy, estate

KEYWORDS: Family, ancestors, ancestry, heritage

MEANINGS

Othala is the rune of family and inheritance, legacy and heritage. This rune showcases and highlights that to which we belong in regard to our family. It is a rune that demonstrates that we are responsible for our heritage, both that which we inherit and that which we pass down. This is your lot in life, all the primal ingredients that make up who you are and what you bring into this life from your family.

In ancient Norse culture, when a leader of an estate passed away, the members of the estate would erect an othal stone. On this stone were carved runes, describing for whom the stone was raised, as well as who raised it. Estates and inheritances were divided by three; a third was buried with the leader, a third went to the funeral, and a third went to the firstborn son, the inheritor of the estate.

Othala is the last rune in the Elder Futhark, and though there is much debate as to whether Dagaz or Othala ends the Elder Futhark, most agree it is Othala. This shows us how important family was to the ancient Norse, and should still be considered today. All of the runes that preceded it—from Fehu to Gebo to Wunjo—show us the culmination of energies. To the Norse, there was no greater success than a well-established and abundant farm, family, and community. All of the energies of the runes lead up to this. Othala shows us a connection to our ancestors and all that we have gained from them.

This is a rune of inheritance and kinship, the clan stronghold. Othala signifies all that is important in loyalty to one's family and tribe. In the sense of Othala, tribe doesn't just mean family. Tribe can mean connection to any group or organization to which you belong: religious, social, school, work, etc. In all things, we must remember the inheritance of the ancestors who came before us. We all come from ancestors who struggled and fought to get us to this day. They didn't have hospitals, grocery stores, doctors, or any other modern conveniences that we take for granted. This means we have a responsibility to ourselves, our families, and our communities to bring the gifts we bear both to our tribe and to the world at large.

Othala can represent the physical inheritance from our family, as well as the financial. It can even signify orlog, the luck and Wyrd that is passed down from parent to child. When Othala shows up in a reading, it is encouraging you to remember that which you've inherited, and to keep in mind the tribe or family of which you are a part.

In all things, we must honor our ancestors by trying to make the world a better place, as much as we can, for our tribe and the world in general. To live a self-absorbed and selfish life dishonors our ancestors and their struggles; Othala reminds us of that.

IN MAGIC

You can use Othala in a magical sense to fortify and strengthen all that's concerned with your family and heritage. Use this rune to solidify family ties, and when used in conjunction with Algiz, it can ward the threshold of your home. Invoke and chant Othala to channel your ancestors.

OTHALA IN RUNELORE

The family building in ancient Norse culture was the longhouse. This was the headquarters of sorts for the family as they worked their farm, growing crops and taking care of livestock. Families were made up of several different smaller family units, and most of what we know about families in the Norse age comes from the Icelandic sagas. This large family, made up of several couples of men and women and their children, helped shape Norse culture at large. These couplings of men and women most likely included a blood relative in one couple related to one other person in all the other couples.

Often times, if people were not cremated at death, they were buried with some of the items they used in daily life. Rich men were sometimes buried in ships, and they might be buried with slaves, weapons, horses, and other goods. This shows us that physical wealth was so valued that it was important to be buried with it.

The Quest Ahead

We've come to the end of our journey, and I want to thank you for joining me. Now you're more familiar with the magic and the mysteries of the runes, and yet I'd like to remind you that this is just the beginning of a lifelong quest to better understand these potent powers of the Universe.

Together we have discovered the mythology of the ancient Norse. We have met the great gods and goddesses of the Aesir and the Vanir, we have traveled with Odin, we have struggled with Thor, and we have witnessed the magnificent benevolence of Freya and Freyr. We have discovered the history of the runes through the ages, and how they've transformed in different time periods throughout our history. You now know how to create your own set of runes, how to cast them, and how to bring them to bear for those around you. You should be proud of yourself, as this wisdom can only make you stronger, and life a little bit easier for you.

Please, keep your rune journal close by. I personally discovered so much about the runes by journaling constantly about them. Part of my morning routine is to pull a rune, asking Odin to show me how my day will unfold, what I should look out for, and of what I should be aware. The runes have been a steadfast, incredible collection of allies that have made my life easier, helping me cultivate energies around situations where I normally would have struggled, yet I found the ability to persevere with their assistance. Journal about your morning rune pull, and journal about rune spreads you do for yourself, friends, and family. Take walks in nature as often as you can, looking for runes in the trees, stones, and waterways around you. Look for runes in the clouds over your head. Journal and document as much as you can about how they interact with your life.

As Odin quested for the runes, and still quests through the nine worlds of Yggdrasil today, so shall you continue your quest for knowledge and wisdom, both in yourself and in the world around you. I encourage you to continue pulling a rune every day. I encourage you to pull runes when you have a question about a struggle or roadblock in your life. I encourage you to create your own set of runes, and I want you to use these exciting energies to help your friends, family, and loved ones find the clarity they need to make it through the challenges of life here on Midgard. The runes have helped me discover so much about the world around me, and even more important, have helped me discover so much about myself.

I only hope this is the first step in the same kind of journey for you.

Resources

Odin: Ecstasy, Runes, & Norse Magic by Diana L. Paxson

+ This fantastic volume helps bring Odin to a modern audience in a very accessible way. It's a great exploration of his history and how he appears in mythology and modern media. Paxson includes a great variety of rituals, exercises, and music so we can all better understand and come to know this profoundly complex god.

Song of the Vikings: Snorri and the Making of Norse Myths by Nancy Marie Brown

+ This book reveals the life and times of Snorri Sturluson, showing him to be as unruly as the gods he put down on paper. This is the story of the man who brought us the *Prose* and *Poetic Eddas* and helps us understand his life, his environs, and his culture, which all better help us understand the stories he brought forth.

Vitki Musings: Runes, Seidr, and Esoteric Asatru: Thoughts of a Norse Sorcerer or Shaman by Kurt Hoogstraat

+ I've taken wonderful classes with Kurt and he's helped me on my journey, from better understanding the runes to working in trance and traveling the Nine Worlds. This book is an invaluable guide to helping one understand the inner and outer workings of the runes within themselves, as well as a better understanding of what modern Asatru can look like.

The Seed of Yggdrasill by Maria Kvilhaug

+ An extensive volume of research and translations of Old Norse myths by an author who has spent most of her life becoming an expert in her field. This book is incredibly enlightening and provides a treasure trove of information, an exciting exploration of all things Norse. This book will not only expand your horizons but also challenge what you think you know, and what you've come to learn.

Northern Mysteries and Magick: Runes & Feminine Powers by Freya Aswynn

- When this book was first published in 1998, it broke new ground and instantly became a classic. This guide brings forth Aswyn's knowledge and expertise of both the runes and the gods and goddesses of the Norse. This book also helps you to explore shamanic drumming, chanting, and journeying and offers great explorations of runes in magick, with charms and sigils to accompany. Highly recommended!

The Prose Edda by Snorri Sturluson

- This work is one of the most well-known and beloved works of Scandinavian literature and has become the most turned-to source for Norse mythology. The stories within have become our best-known resource of all the myths of Odin, Thor, and all the other Norse gods.

The Poetic Edda translated by Jackson Crawford

- This other well-known resource of Scandinavian lore features prominent poetry that is considered the other preeminent source of Norse mythology. Here you'll discover the *Völuspá*, the Prophecy of Ragnarok, and the *Hávamál*, the Counsel of Odin the One-Eyed.

The Big Book of Runes and Rune Magic by Edred Thorsson

- Edred Thorsson is known worldwide as one of the best authorities in runology, studying runes and publishing works on runes for decades. This guide offers information on rune lore, guidance for how to interpret runes, and in-depth practices for runic magic and rune casting.

Taking Up the Runes: A Complete Guide to Using Runes in Spells, Rituals, Divination, and Magic by Diana L. Paxson

- This is one of the books that I go back to time and time again, offering in-depth analyses of each rune, as well as fantastic methods for casting rune spells and performing rituals specific to runes.

Nordic Runes by Paul Rhys Mountfort

- This book was one of the easiest and most accessible books that I first read on runes, helping me understand each rune individually. This volume also offers simple reflections of Norse mythology specific to the runes, helping people better understand the origin of the runes.

The Viking Spirit: An Introduction to Norse Mythology and Religion by Daniel McCoy

- This accessible volume is divided into two sections: Norse religion, showing us how the Norse saw gods and goddesses, fate, death, and magic, and Norse mythology, sharing specific tales about the Norse gods and goddesses and their exploits.

References

Books

Crawford, Jackson. *The Poetic Edda: Stories of the Norse Gods and Heroes.* Indianapolis, IN: Hackett Publishing Company, Inc., 2015.

McCoy, Daniel. *The Viking Spirit: An Introduction to Norse Mythology and Religion.* CreateSpace Independent Publishing Platform, 2016.

Mountfort, Paul Rhys. *Nordic Runes: Understanding, Casting, and Interpreting the Ancient Viking Oracle.* Rochester, VT: Destiny Books, 2003.

Olsen, Kaedrich. *Runes for Transformation: Using Ancient Symbols to Change Your Life.* San Francisco, CA: Red Wheel/Weiser, LLC, 2008.

Paxson, Diana L. *Taking Up the Runes: A Complete Guide to Using Runes in Spells, Rituals, Divination, and Magic.* York Beach, ME: Red Wheel/Weiser, LLC, 2005.

Sturluson, Snorri. *The Prose Edda: Translated with an Introduction and Notes by Jesse L. Byock.* London: Penguin Classics, 2005.

Tacitus. *Agricola and Germania.* Edited by James Rives and translated by Harold Mattingly. London: Penguin Classics, 2010.

Thorsson, Edred. *The Big Book of Runes and Rune Magic: How to Interpret Runes, Rune Lore, and the Art of Runecasting.* Newburyport, MA: Weiser Books, 2018.

Websites

Christiansen, Annette Broteng. "The Runic Alphabet – Futhark." *ThorNews.* March 2, 2013. Accessed September 15, 2019. https://thornews.com/2013/03/02/the-runic-alphabet-futhark/.

Cyrus the Strong. "Bind-Rune Basics." *Real Rune Magick*. October 14, 2017. Accessed September 15, 2019. http://realrunemagick.blogspot.com/2017/10 /bind-rune-basics.html.

Hilliard, Bryan. "Futhark: Mysterious Ancient Runic Alphabet of Northern Europe." *Ancient Origins*. August 29, 2019. Accessed September 15, 2019. https://www.ancient-origins.net/artifacts-ancient -writings/futhark-mysterious-ancient-runic-alphabet-northern -europe-003250.

McCoy, Daniel. "Runes." *Norse Mythology for Smart People*. Accessed September 15, 2019. https://norse-mythology.org/Runes/.

McCoy, Daniel. "The Origins of the Runes." *Norse Mythology for Smart People*. Accessed September 15, 2019. https://norse-mythology.org/Runes /the-origins-of-the-Runes/.

McCoy, Daniel. "The Vegvisir." *Norse Mythology for Smart People*. Accessed September 15, 2019. https://norse-mythology.org/vegvisir/.

Mythologian.net. "Vegvisir, The Symbol of Guidance and Protection & Its Meaning–The Viking Compass/Runic Compass." Accessed September 15, 2019. https://mythologian.net/vegvisir-symbol-guidance -protection-meaning-viking-compass-runic-compass/.

Prof. Geller. "Troll." *Mythology.net*. Updated January 19. 2017. Accessed September 15, 2019. https://mythology.net/norse/norse-creatures/troll/.

Short, William R. "Families and Demographics in the Viking Age." *Hurstwic*. Accessed September 15, 2019. http://www.hurstwic.org/history /articles/daily_living/text/Demographics.htm.

Sons of Vikings. "Santa and Odin - Christmas and Yule." December 15, 2017. Accessed September 15, 2019. https://sonsofvikings.com/blogs /history/viking-origins-of-christmas-yule-traditions.

Rune Index

General Index

Acknowledgments

First, I'd like to thank my family for all their support and belief in me, even when I couldn't believe in myself. To my parents for working hard to give me the best life they could. To my son, Sequoia, for making fatherhood one of the easiest joys I've ever experienced. To my husband, Isaac, for boundless love and encouragement, and for helping me see my own potential.

A huge thanks to Vanessa Ta and the friends at Callisto Media, for not only believing in my potential but helping me craft a book that I hope will help countless others in their journey of self-exploration.

Thanks to the friends and mentors I've made along the way: Kurt Hoogstraat, Christina Marvel, and Wylde Hunter, among others. To varying degrees, they've all shown me different aspects of the runes and Norse traditions, helping me discover the endless nuances of the lore, Seidr, and the runes.

To the thousands of clients who have taken a chance on receiving a rune reading from me: This book wouldn't have come about if it weren't for you and your support. I hope I've touched your life as much as you've touched mine.

Also, I would like to thank the gods and goddess who have overseen my journey. From Odin to Freya, from Tyr to Thor, they've all made themselves known in my life in one way or another, and I wouldn't be where I am without them.

And to the runes themselves, I thank them for their magic and mystery. May they always be by my side. May they always find their way into the lives of others. And may the lives of others be forever changed for the better by their influence.

About the Author

Born and raised in northern New England, psychic medium Josh Simonds discovered his gifts years ago when the research into his ancestry coalesced with his personal discovery of the runes. Upon discovery of his ancestral roots in the Nordic and Celtic worlds, he began studying the runes in earnest. Since then, he's provided psychic readings and mediumship sessions using the runes to thousands across the globe. Find him online at JoshSimonds.com.

CPSIA information can be obtained
at www.ICGtesting.com
Printed in the USA
BVHW010158110723
667040BV00003B/27